THE ART OF

MICHAEL FOUNTAIN

VOLUME 1

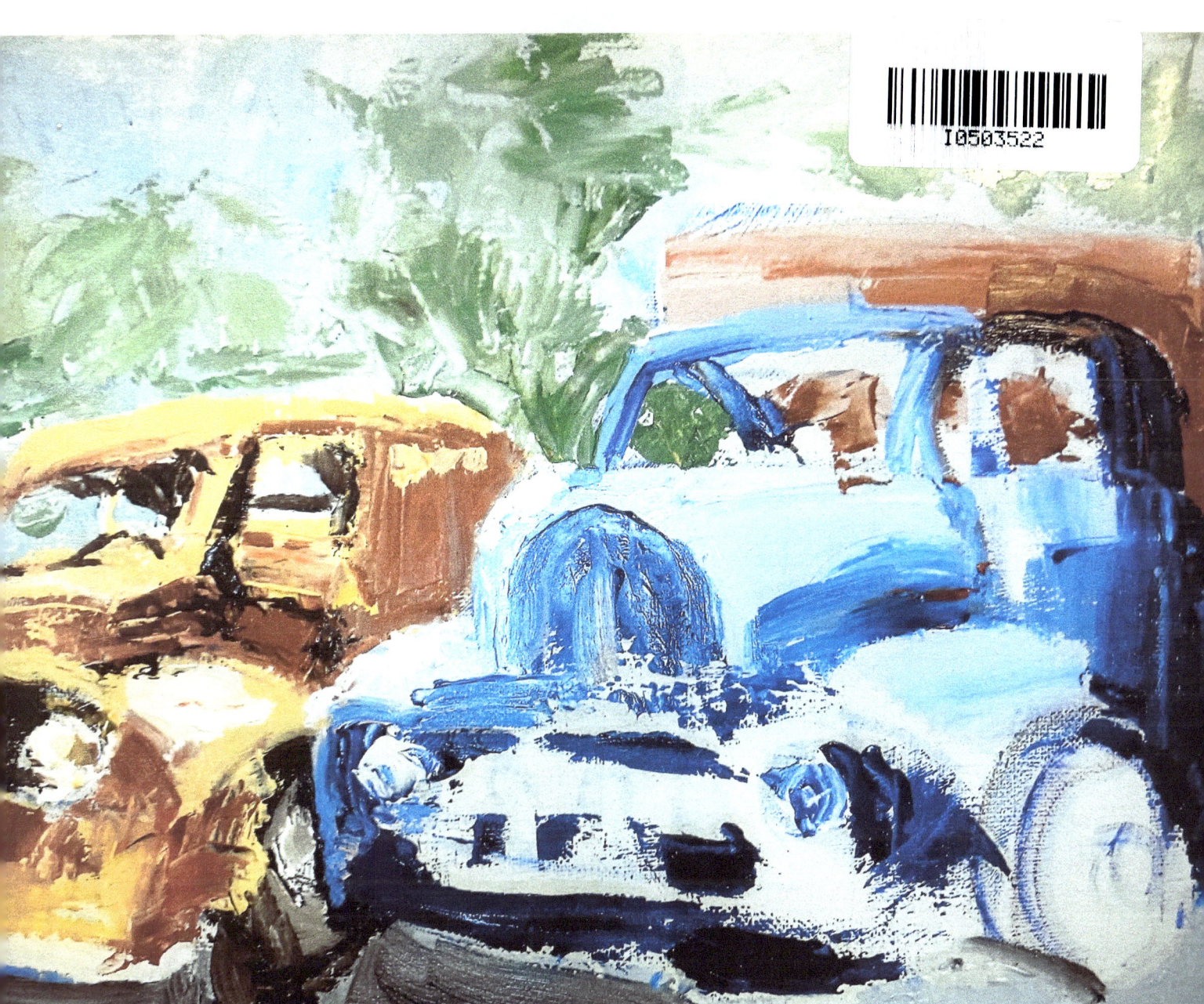

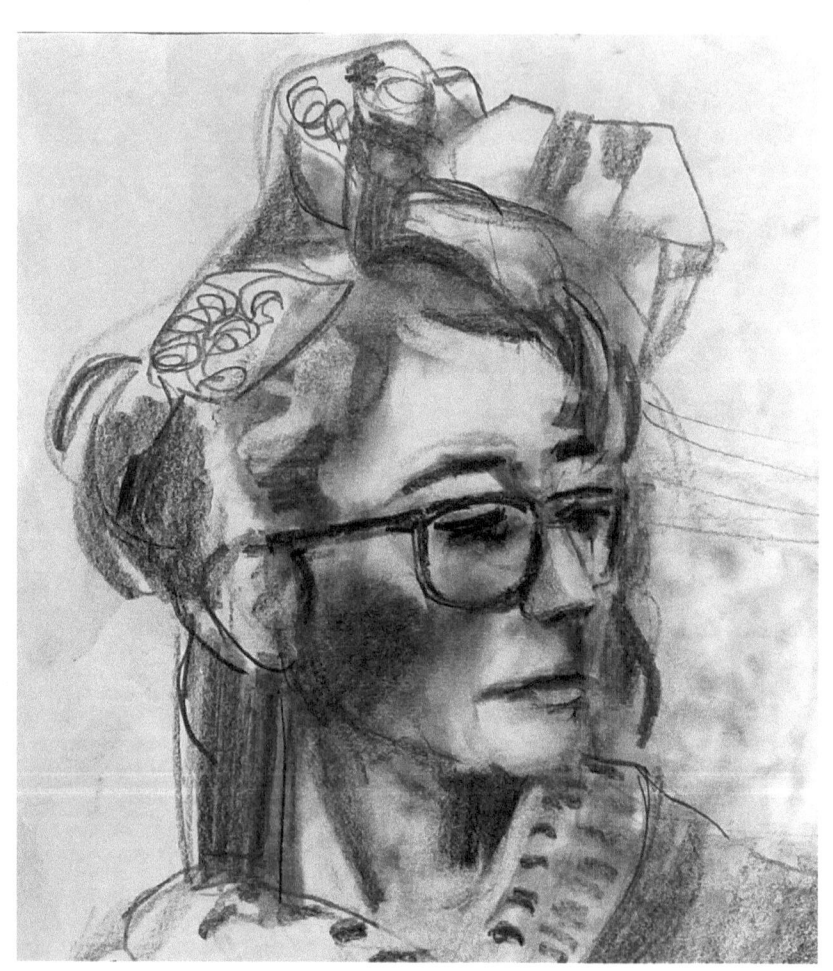

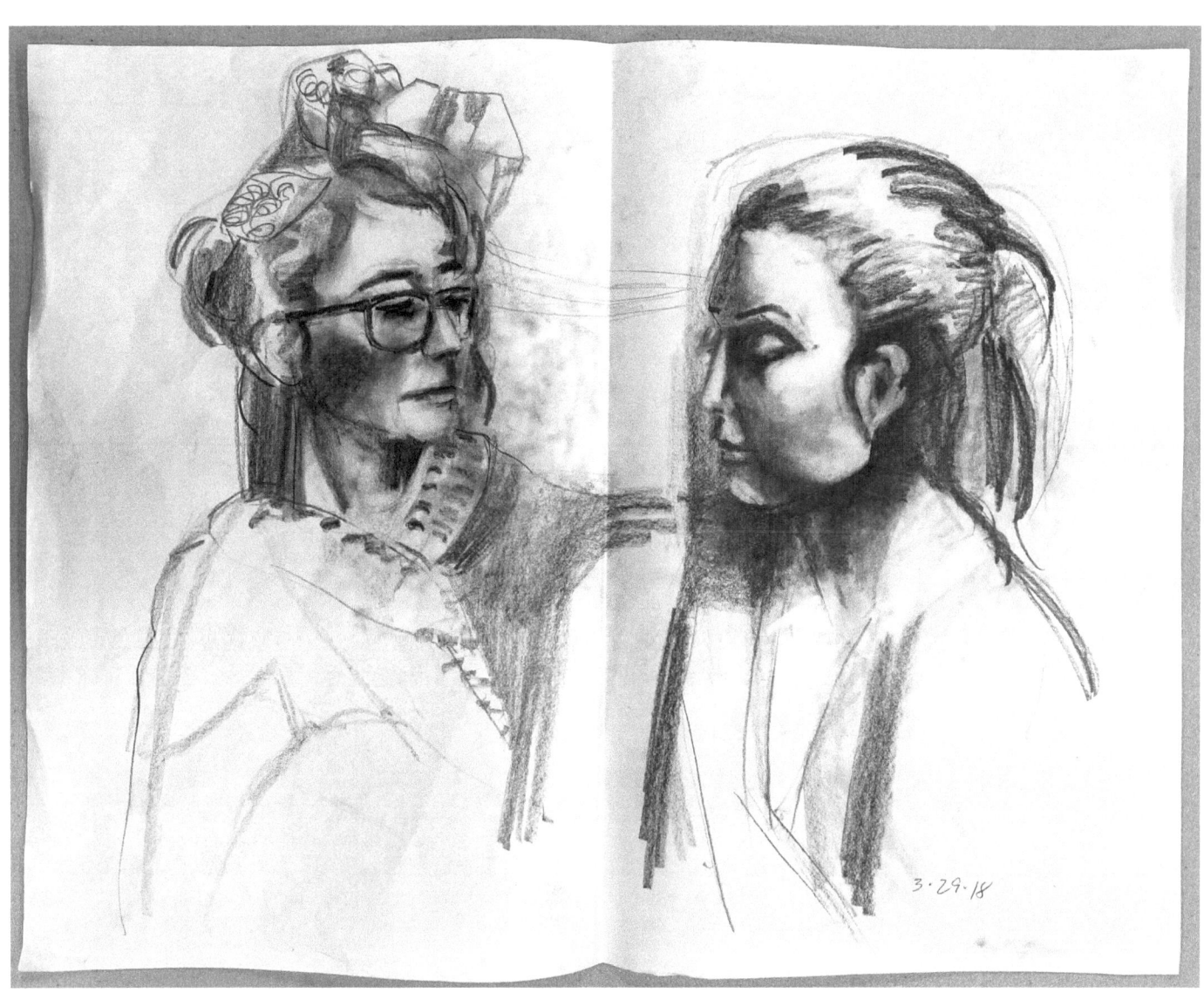

3·29·18

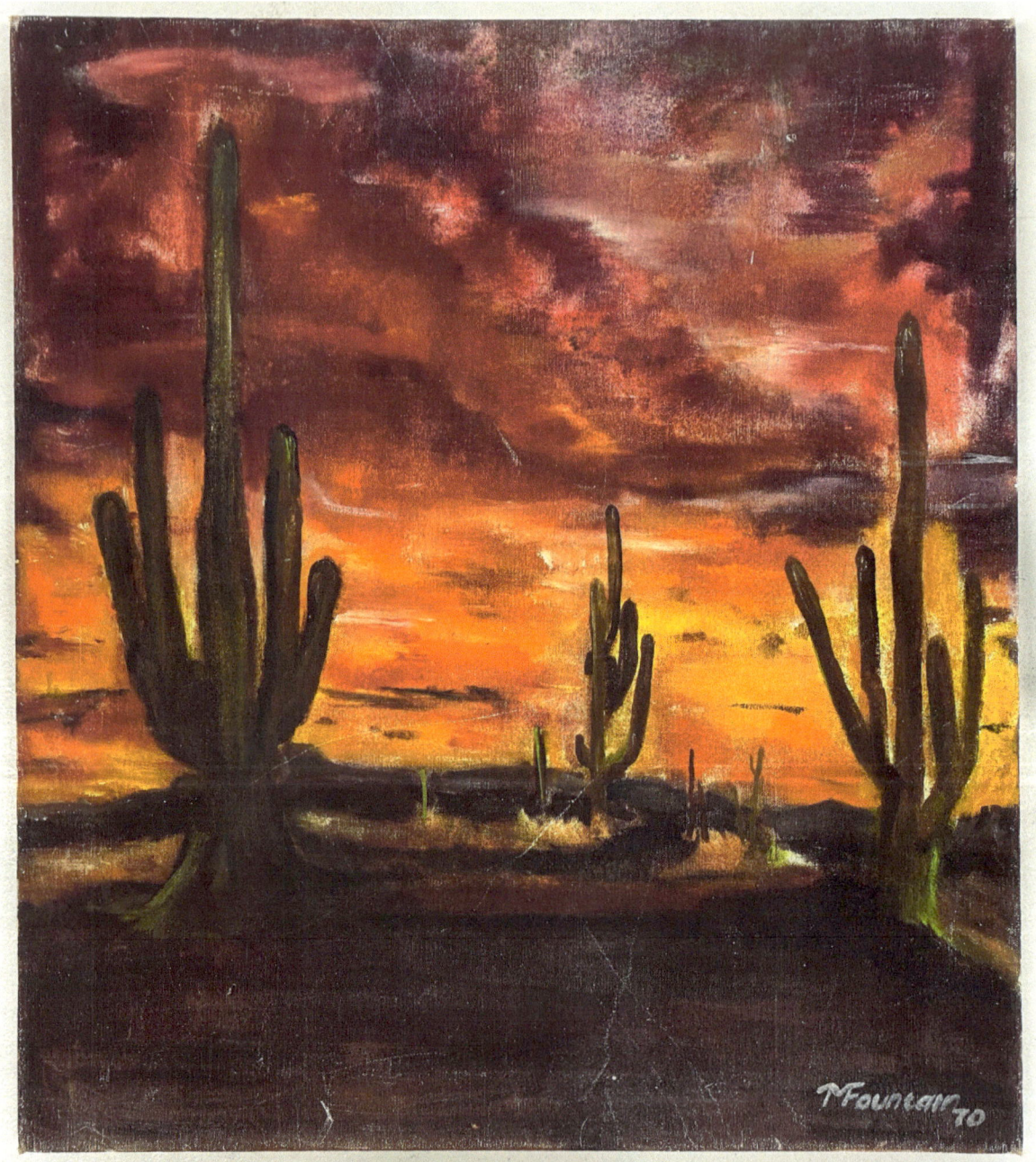

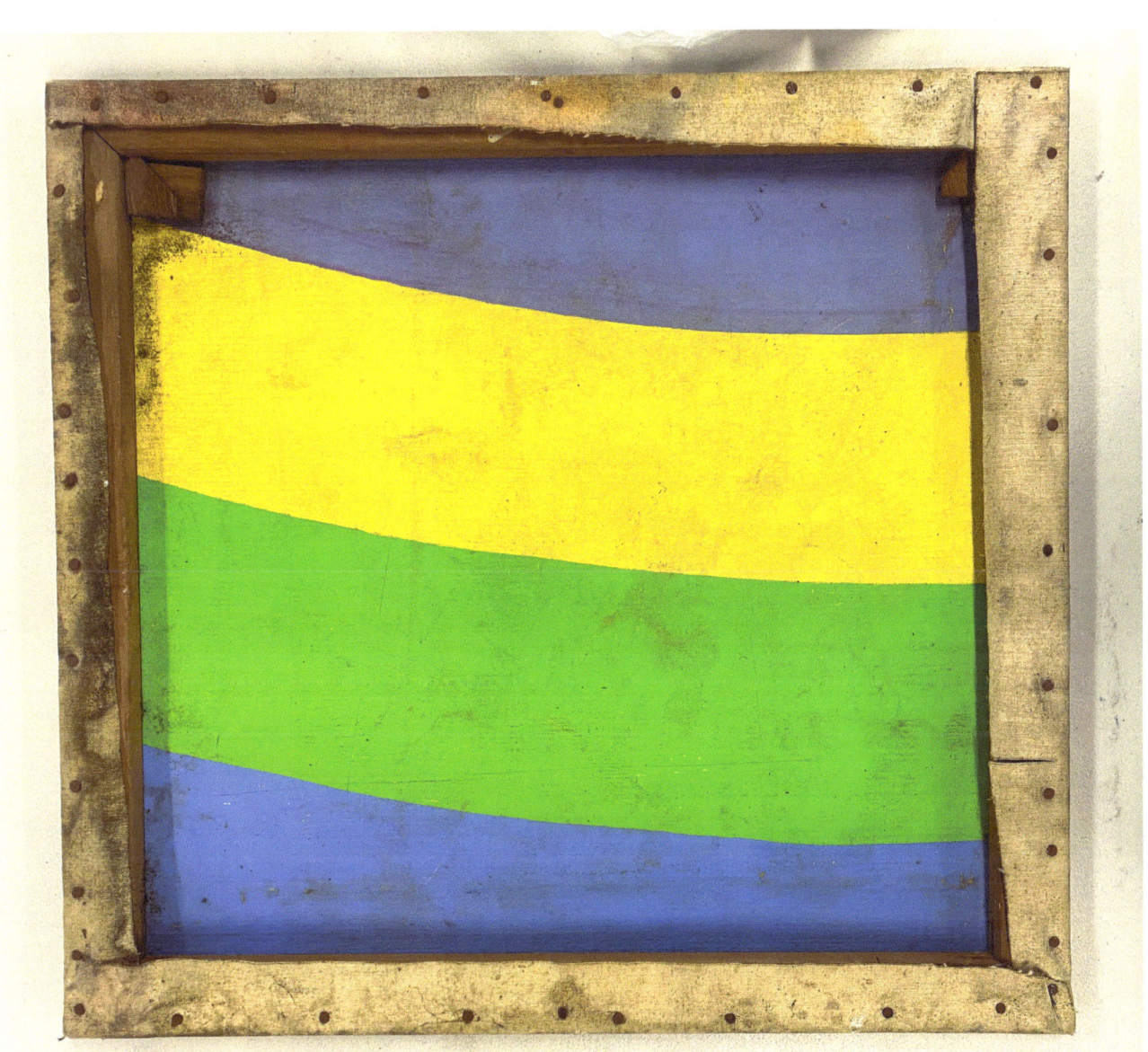

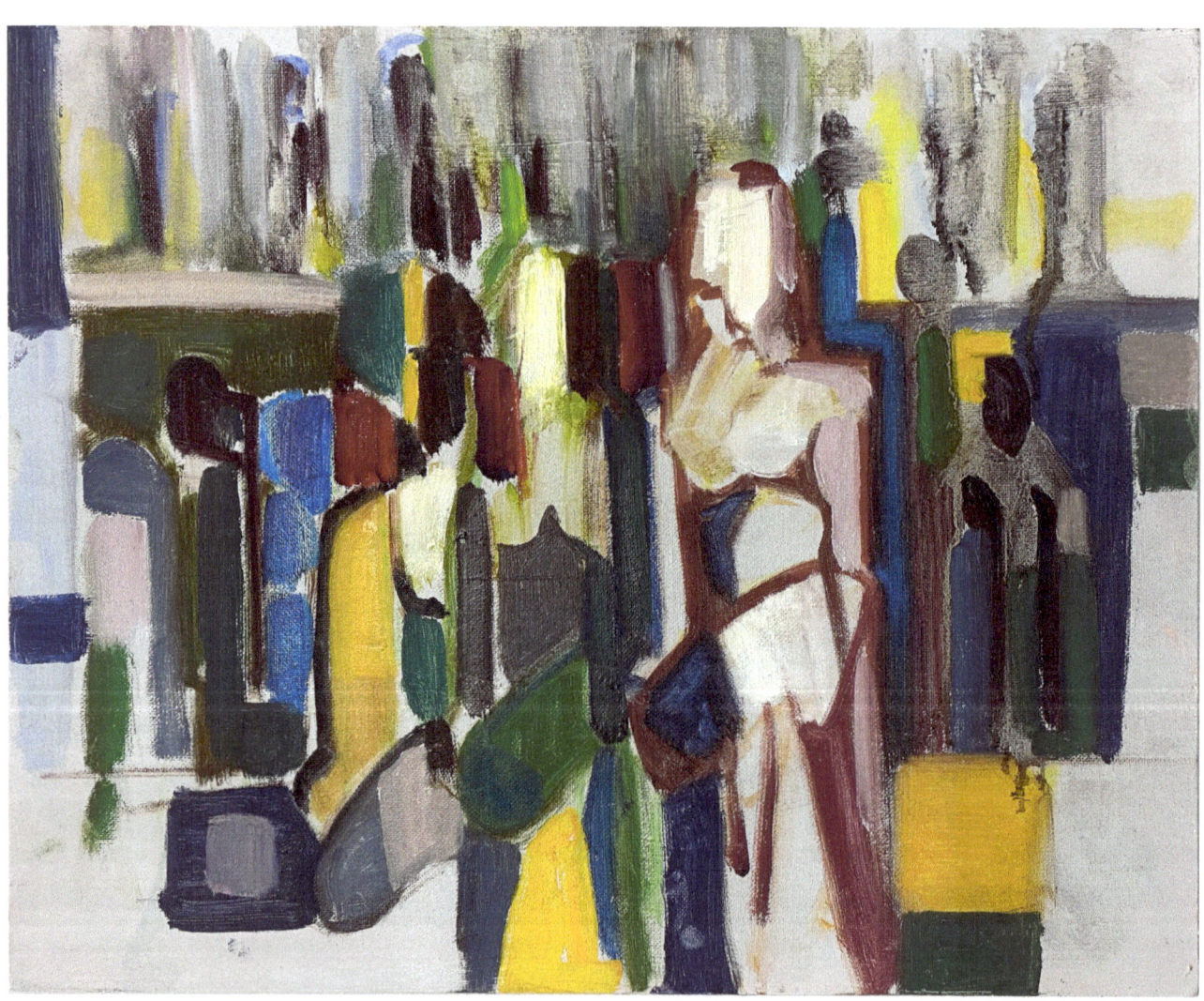

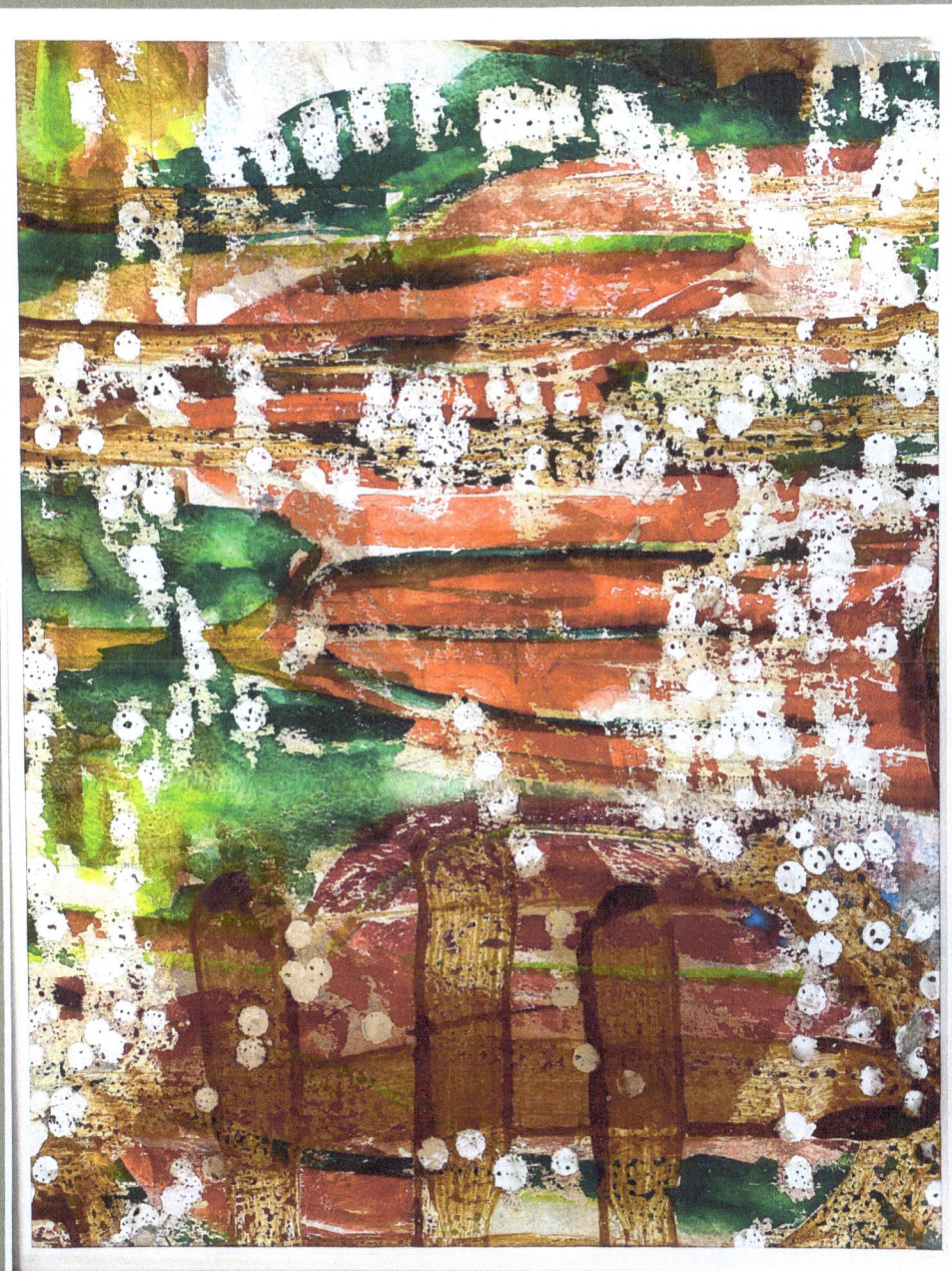

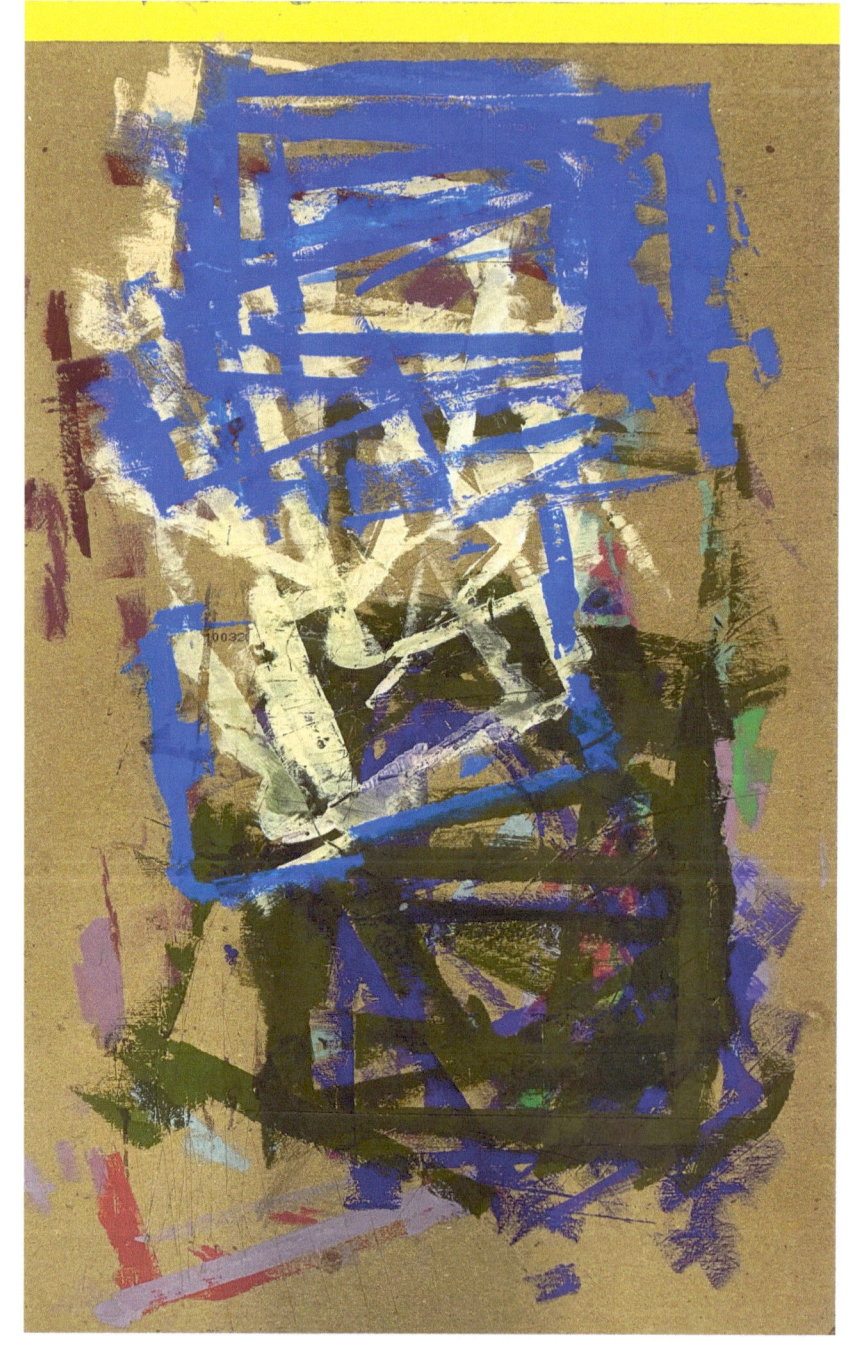

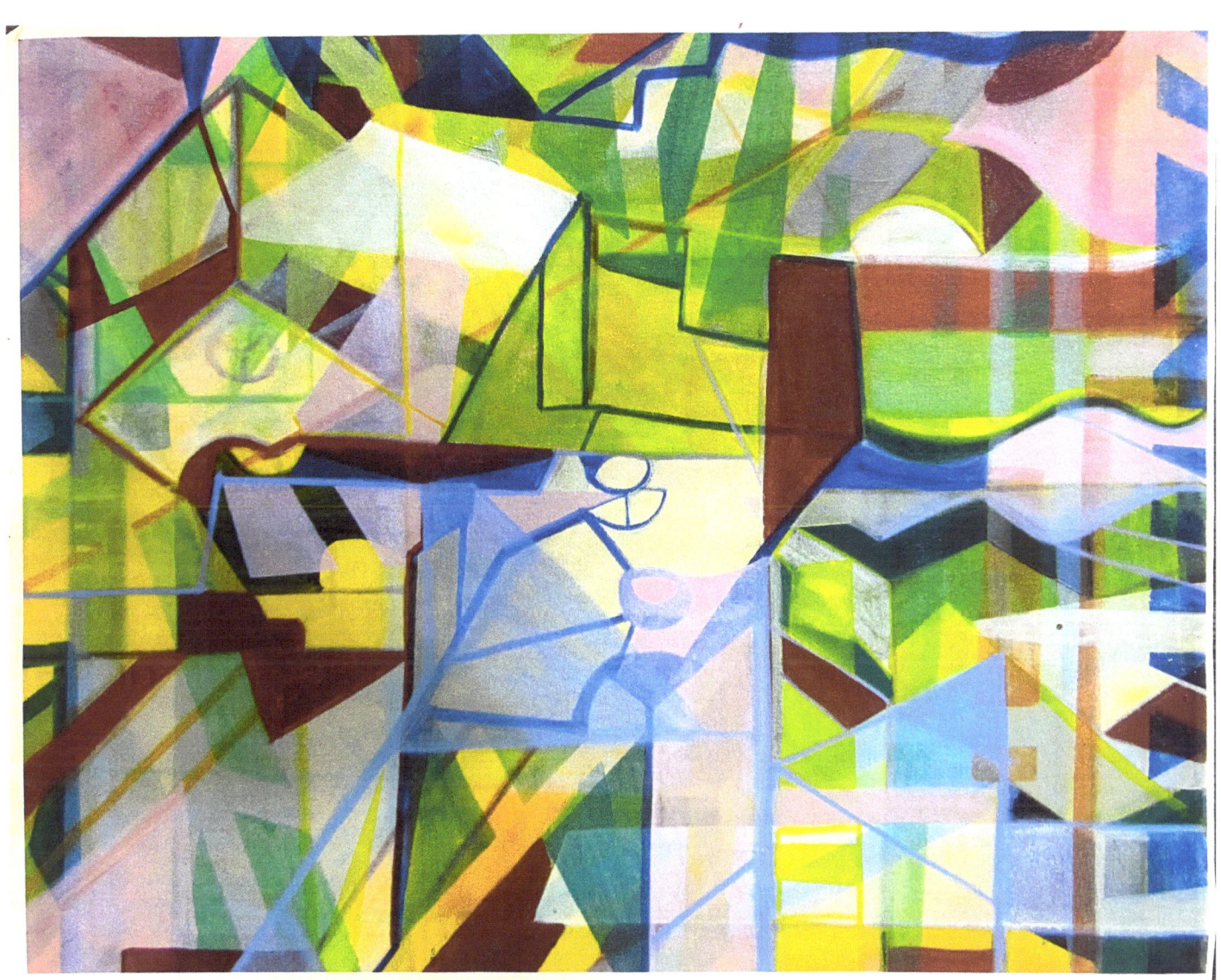

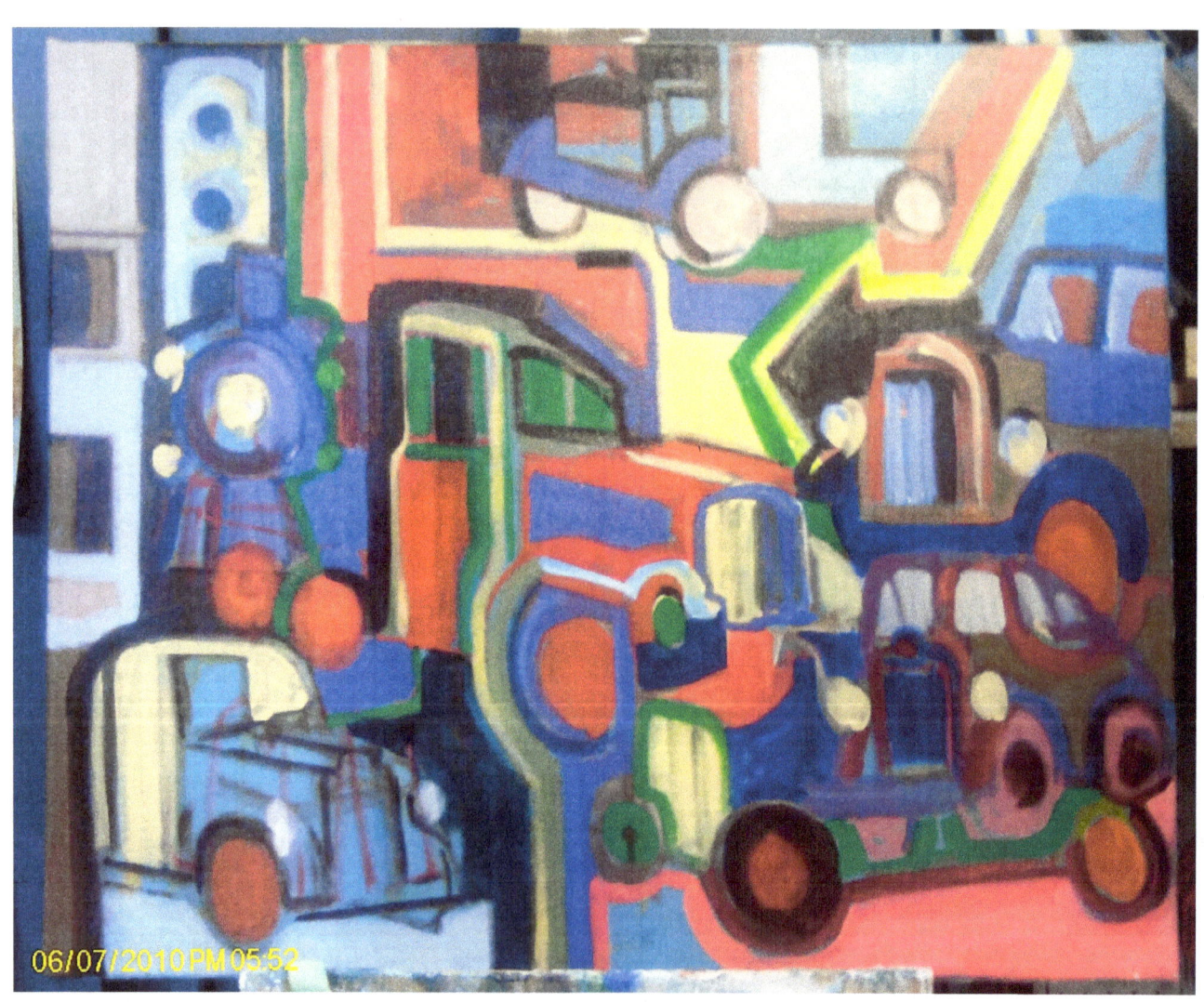
06/07/2010 PM 05:52

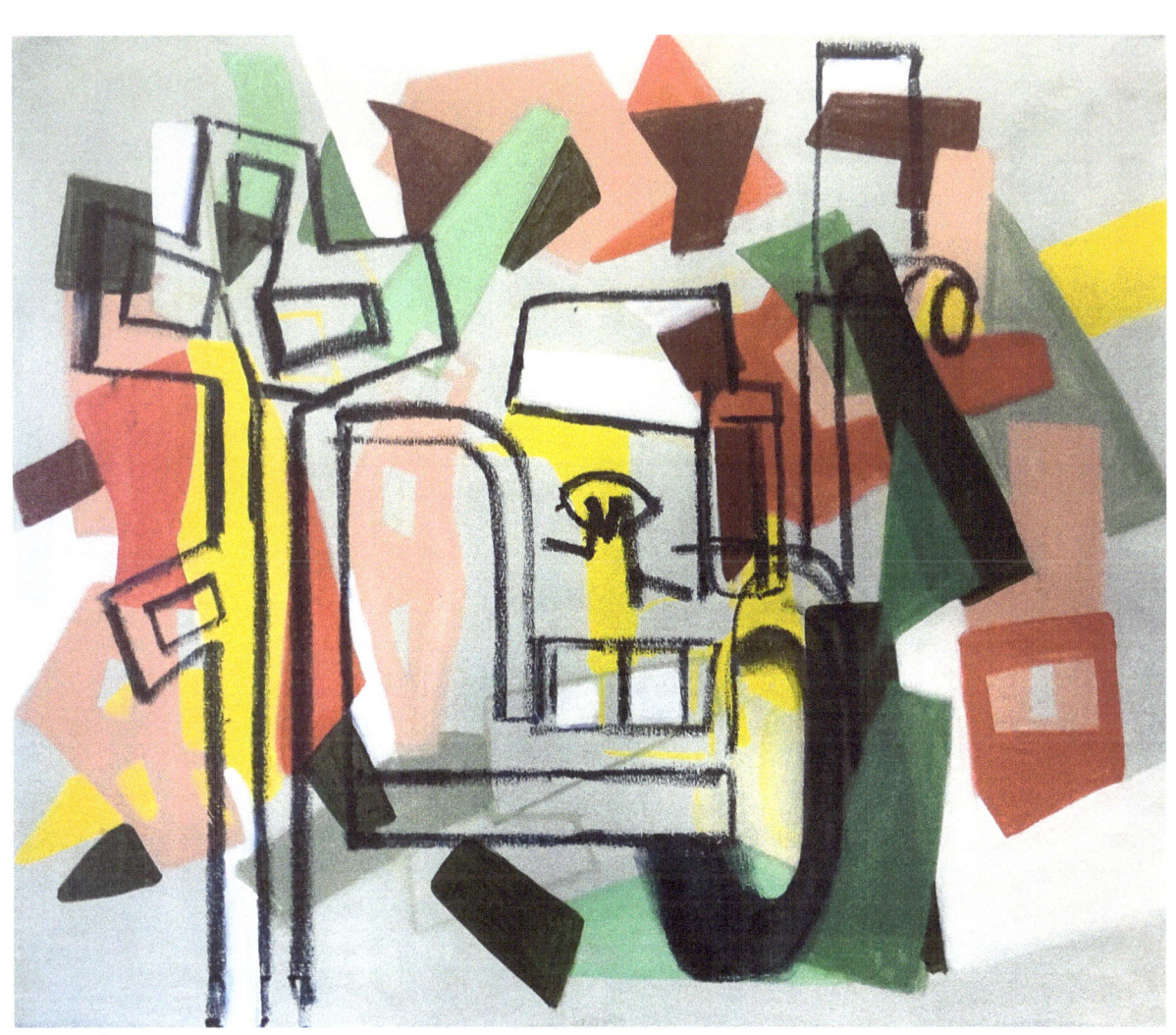

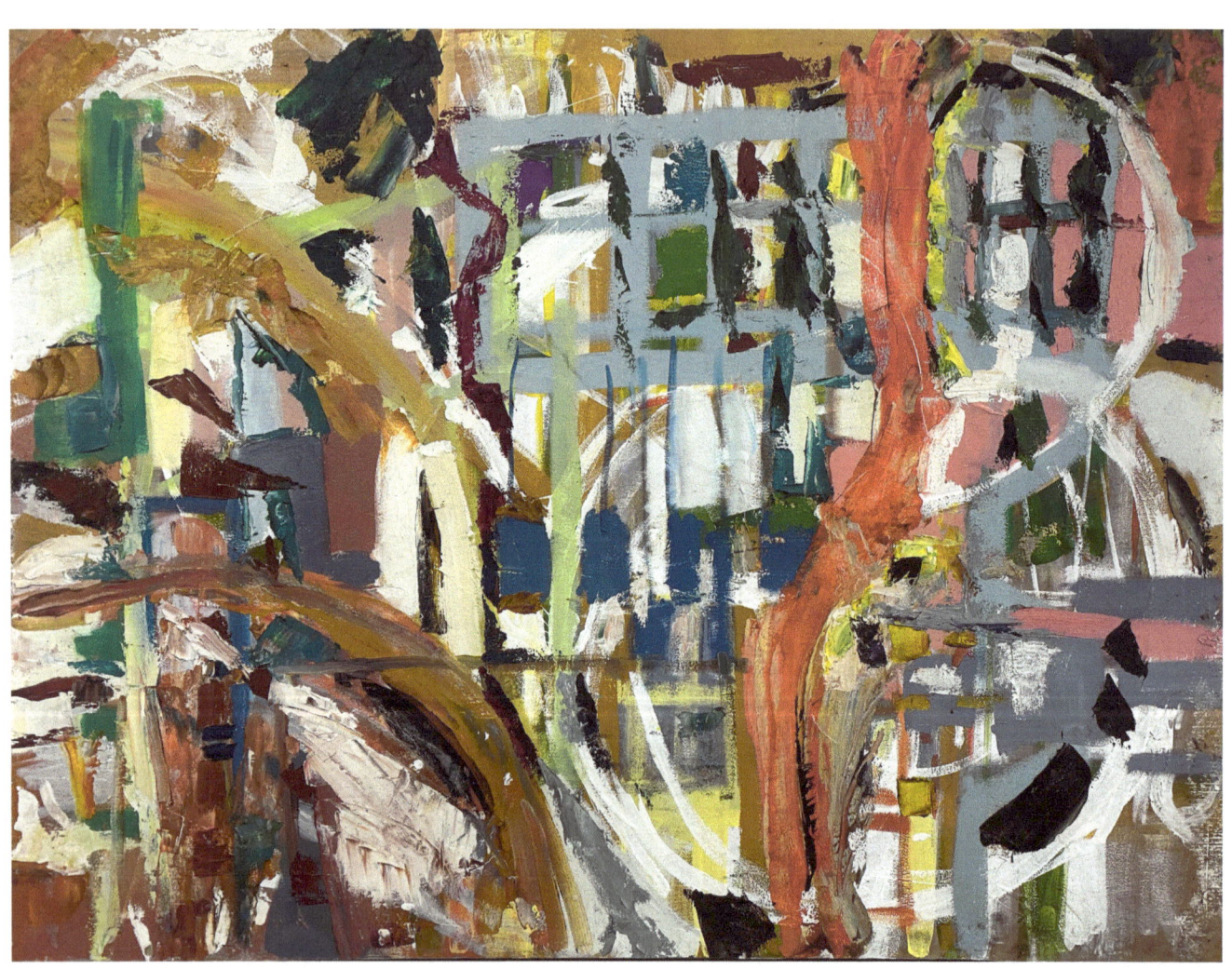

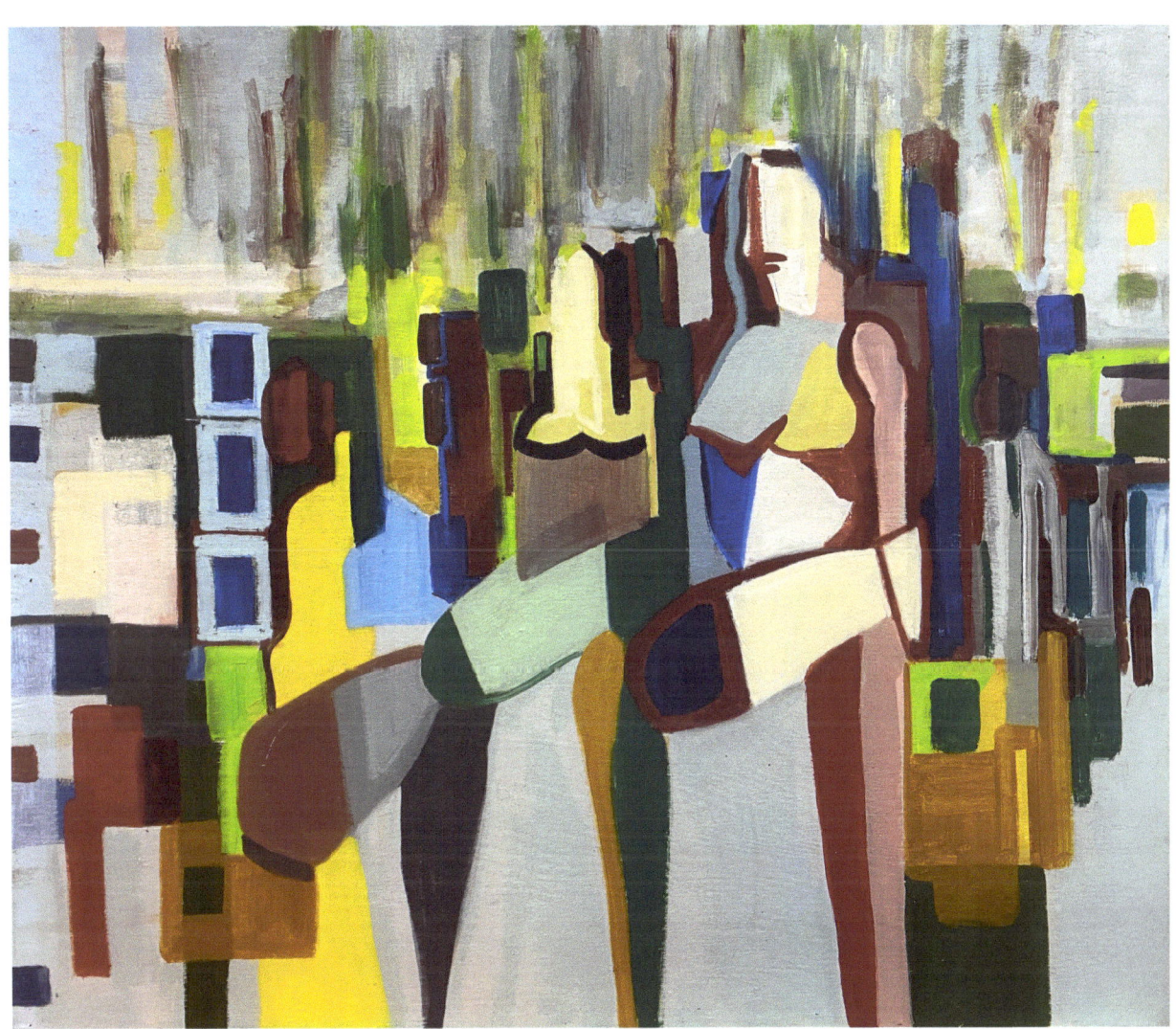

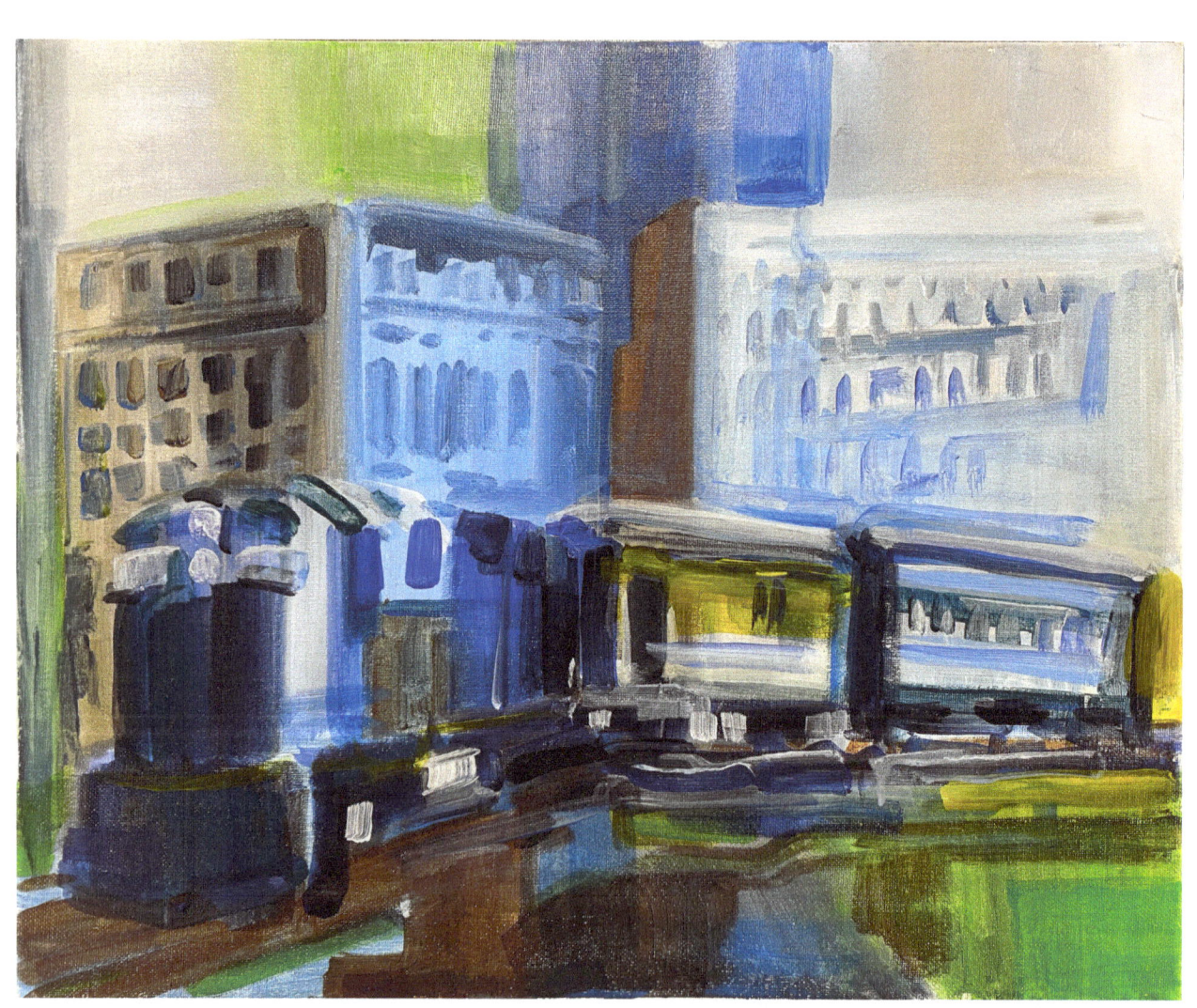

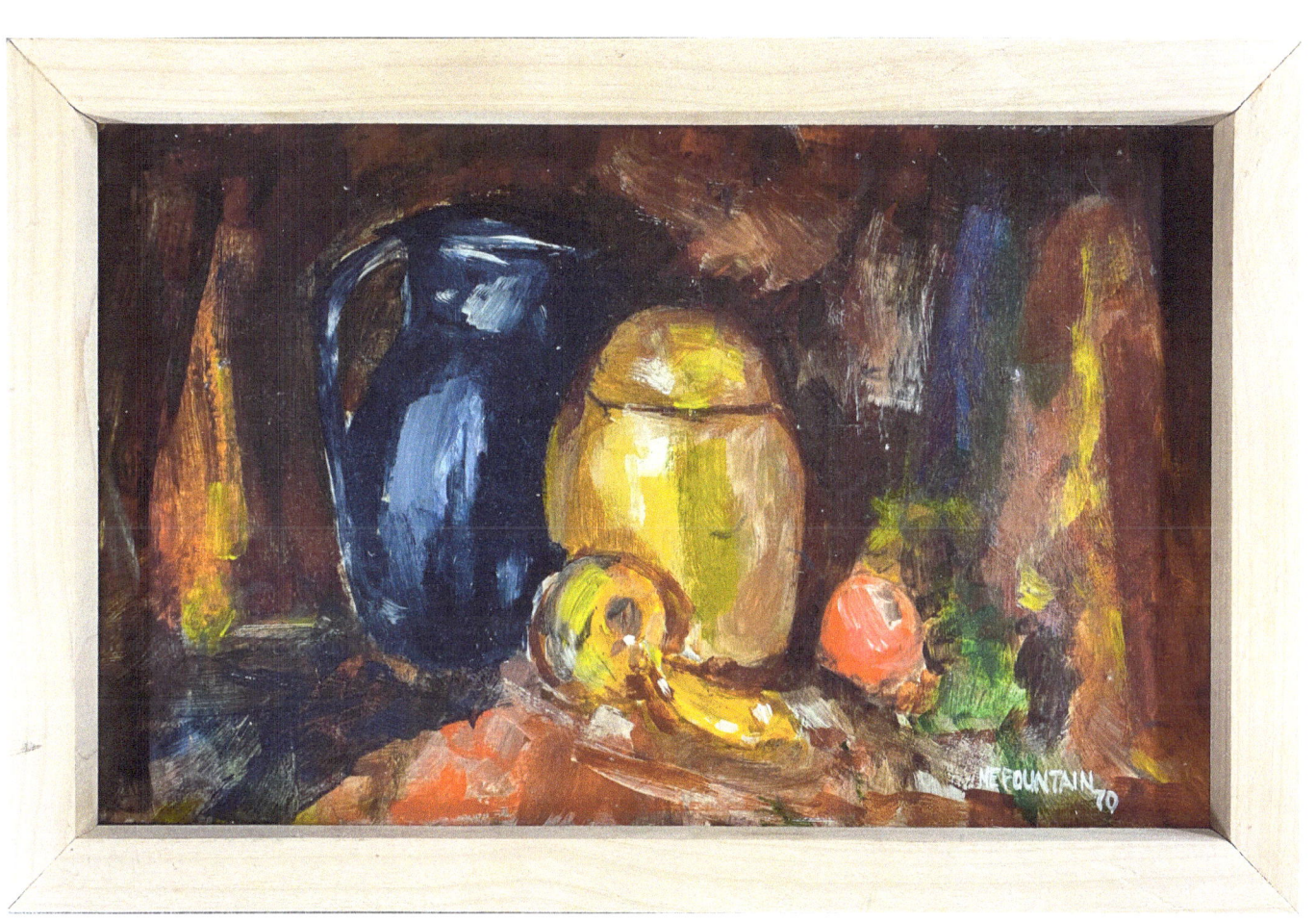

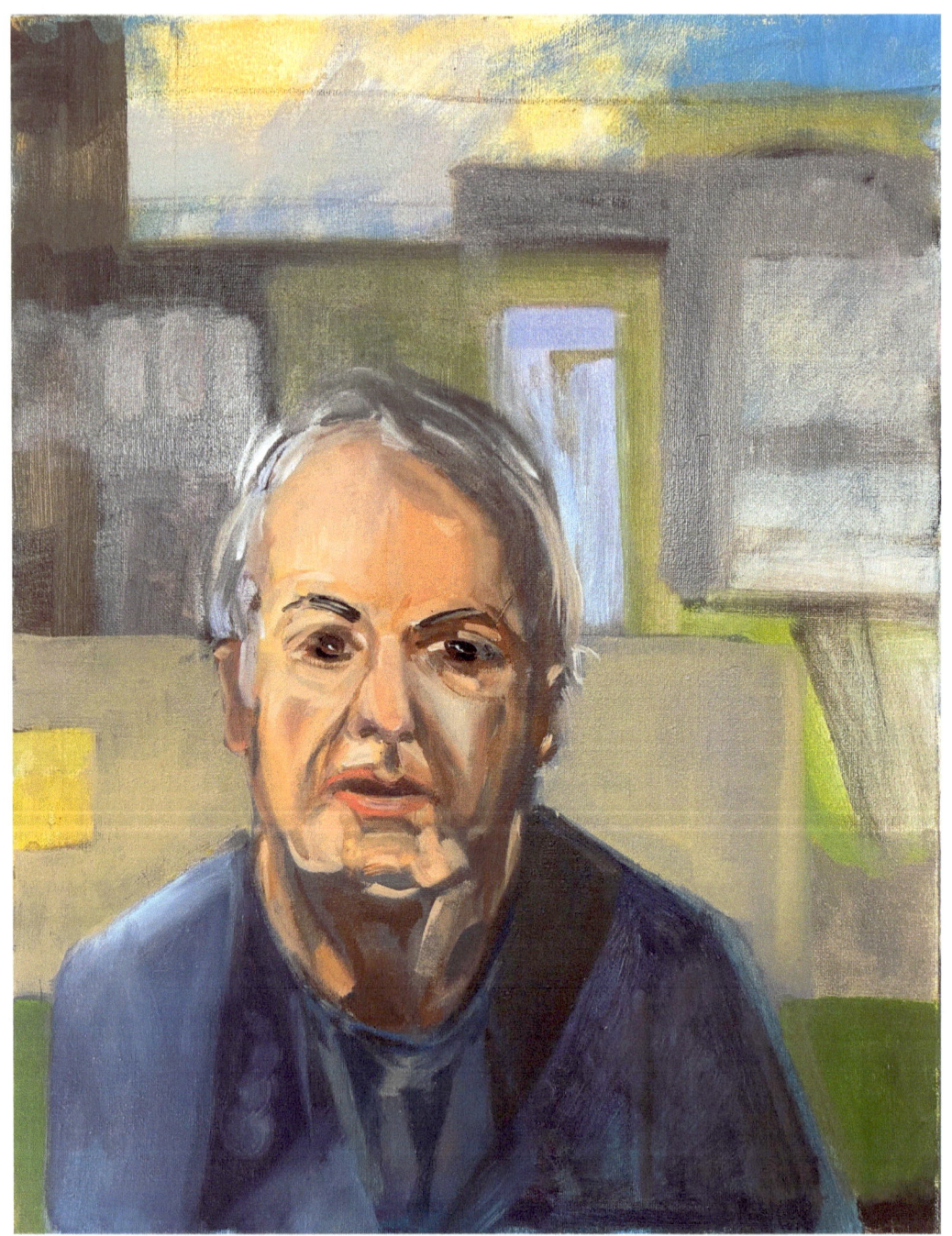

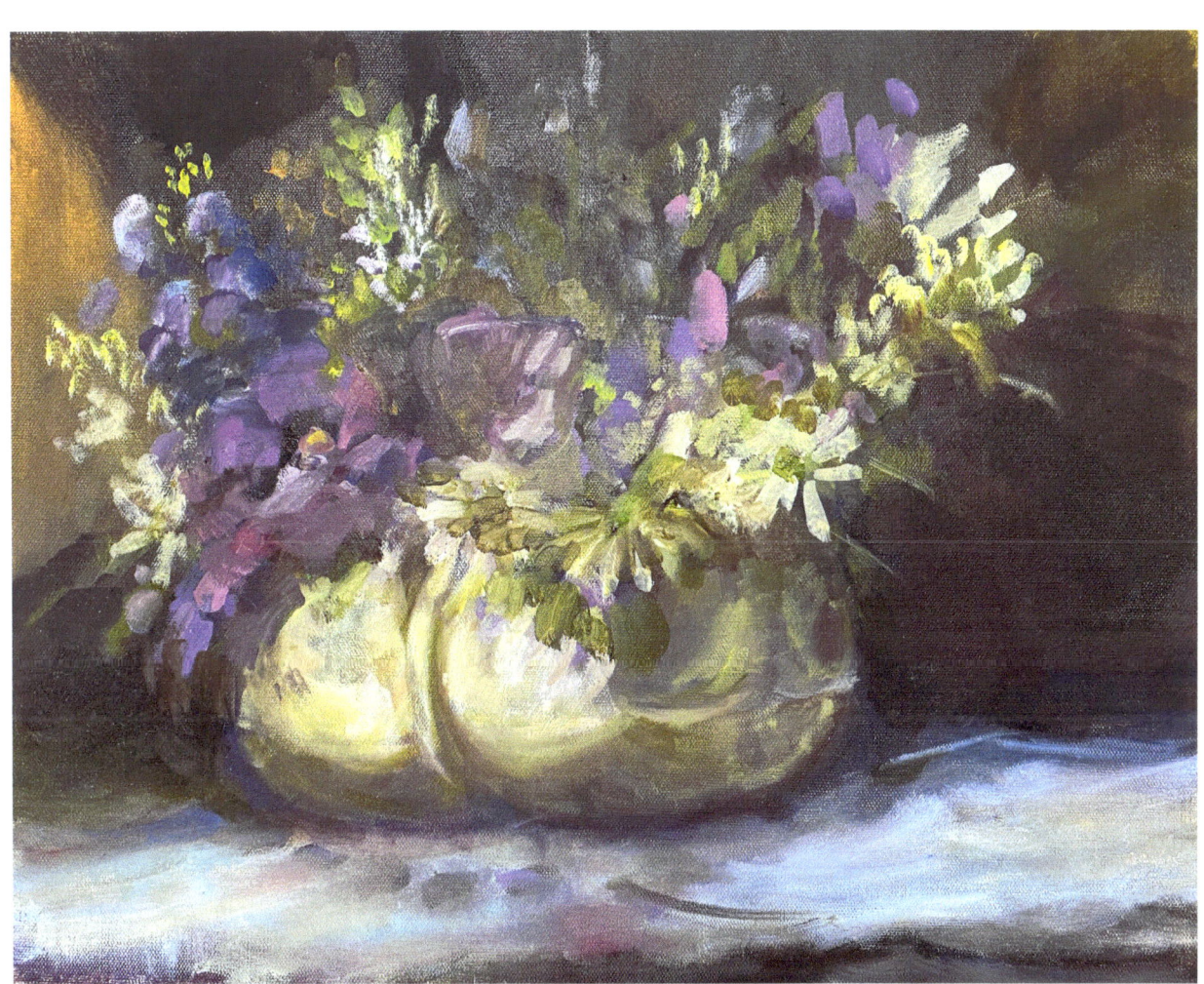

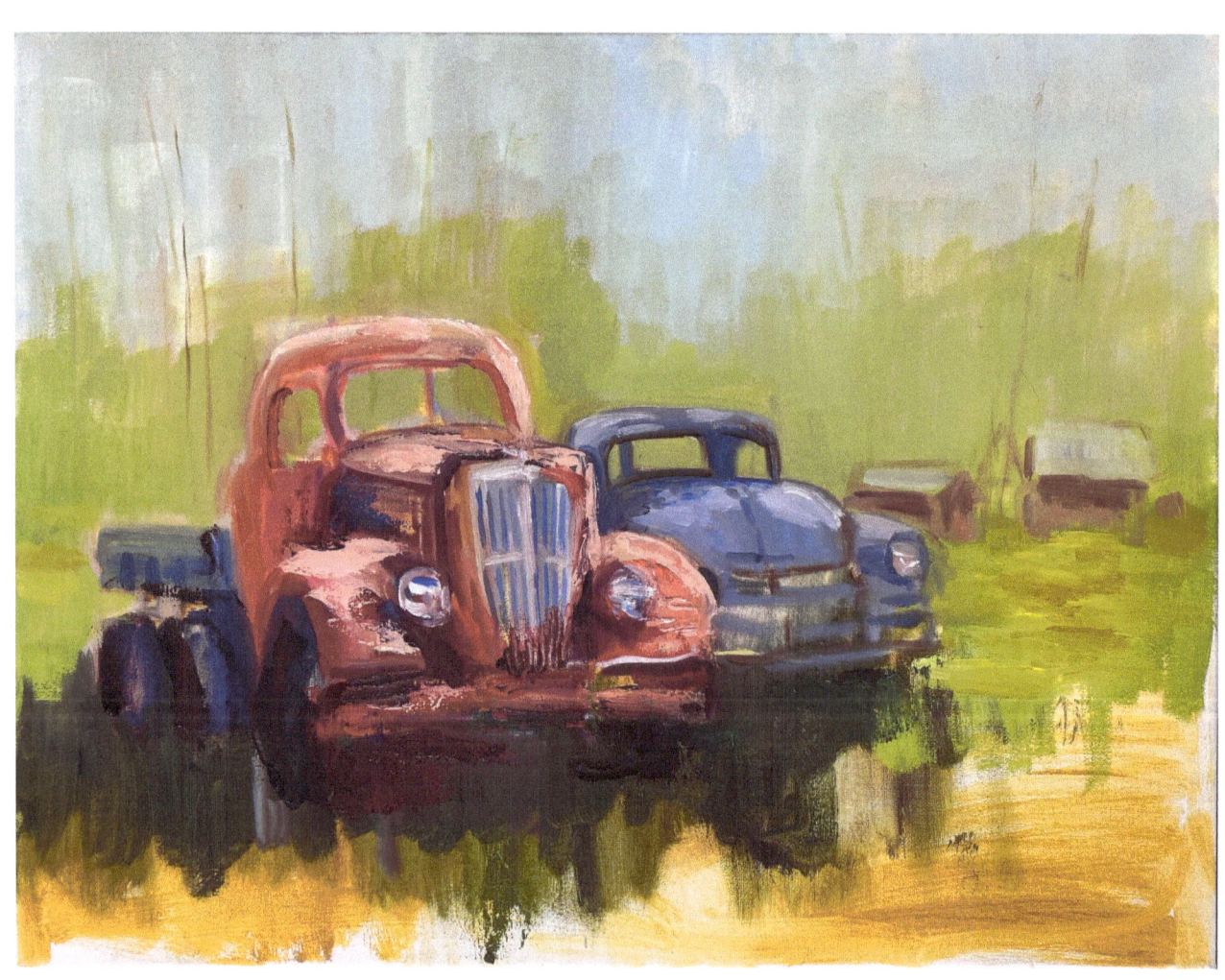

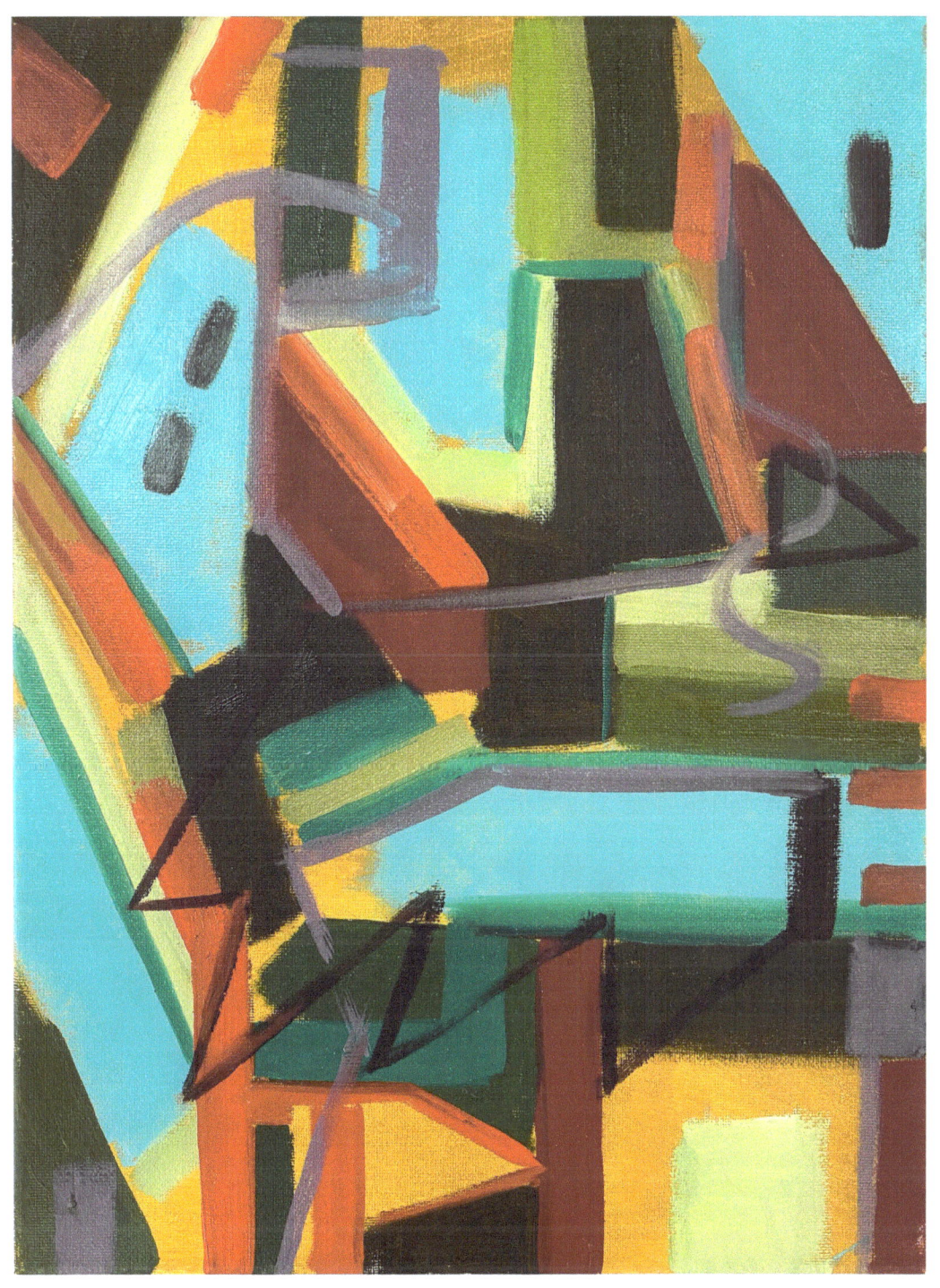

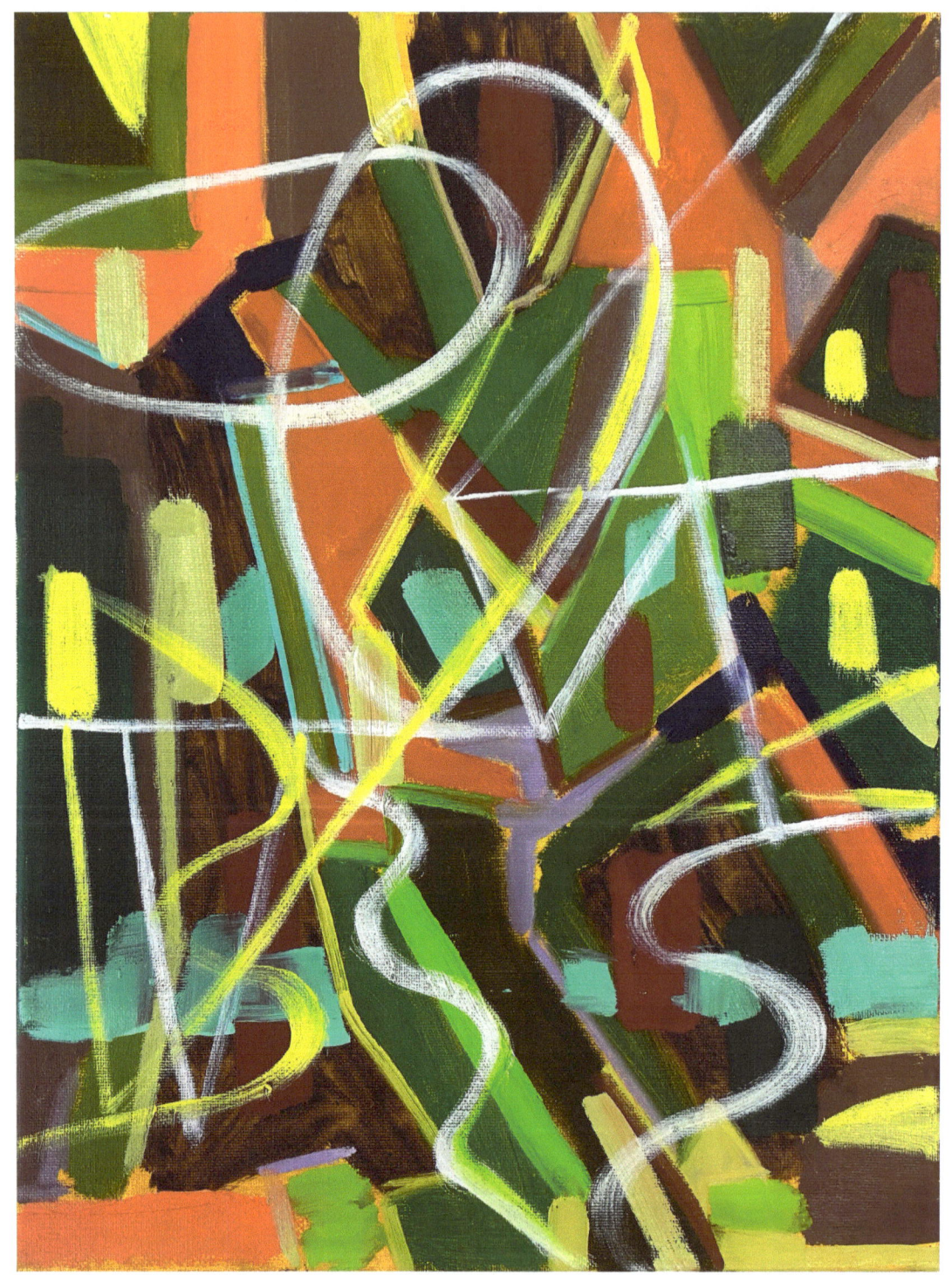

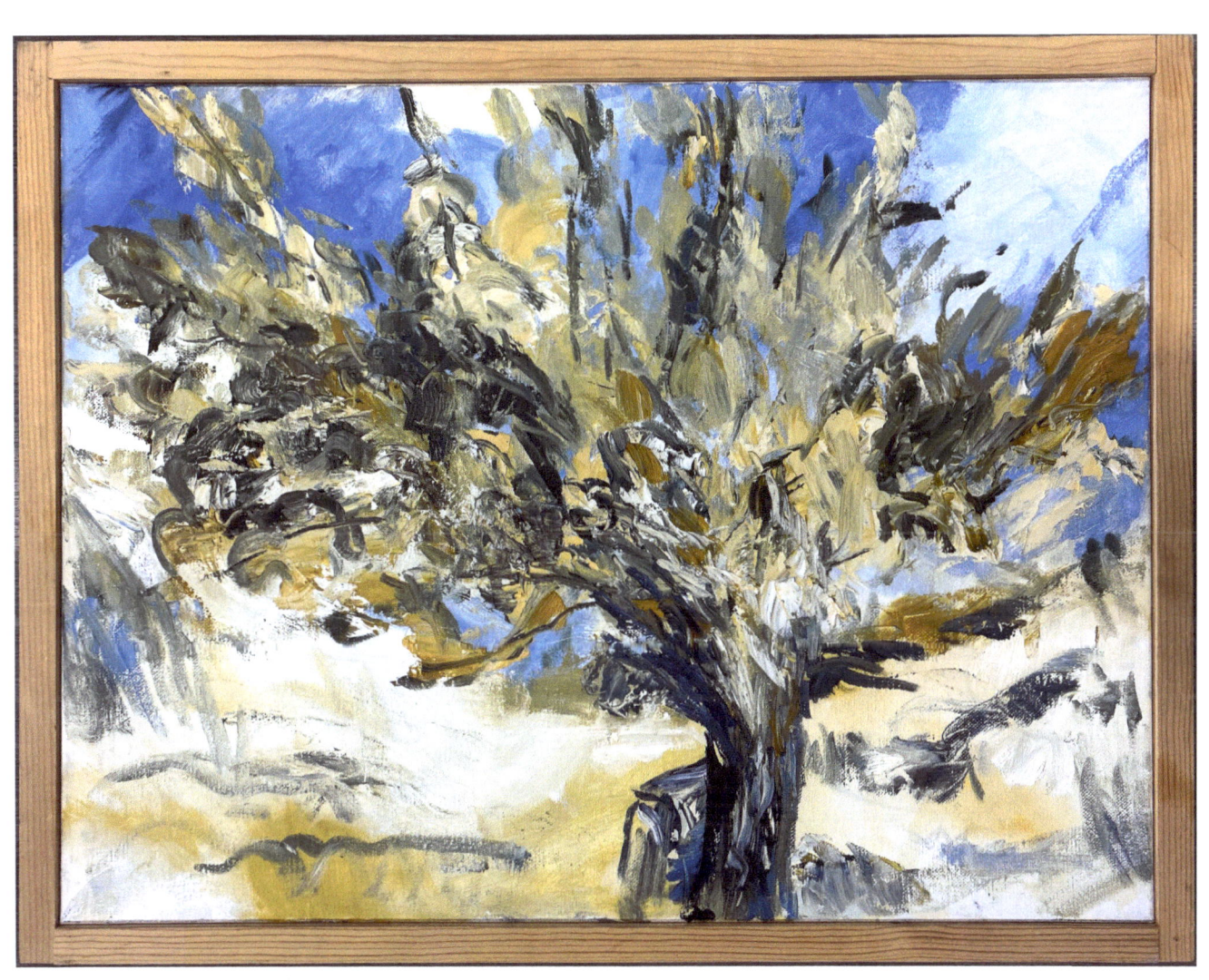

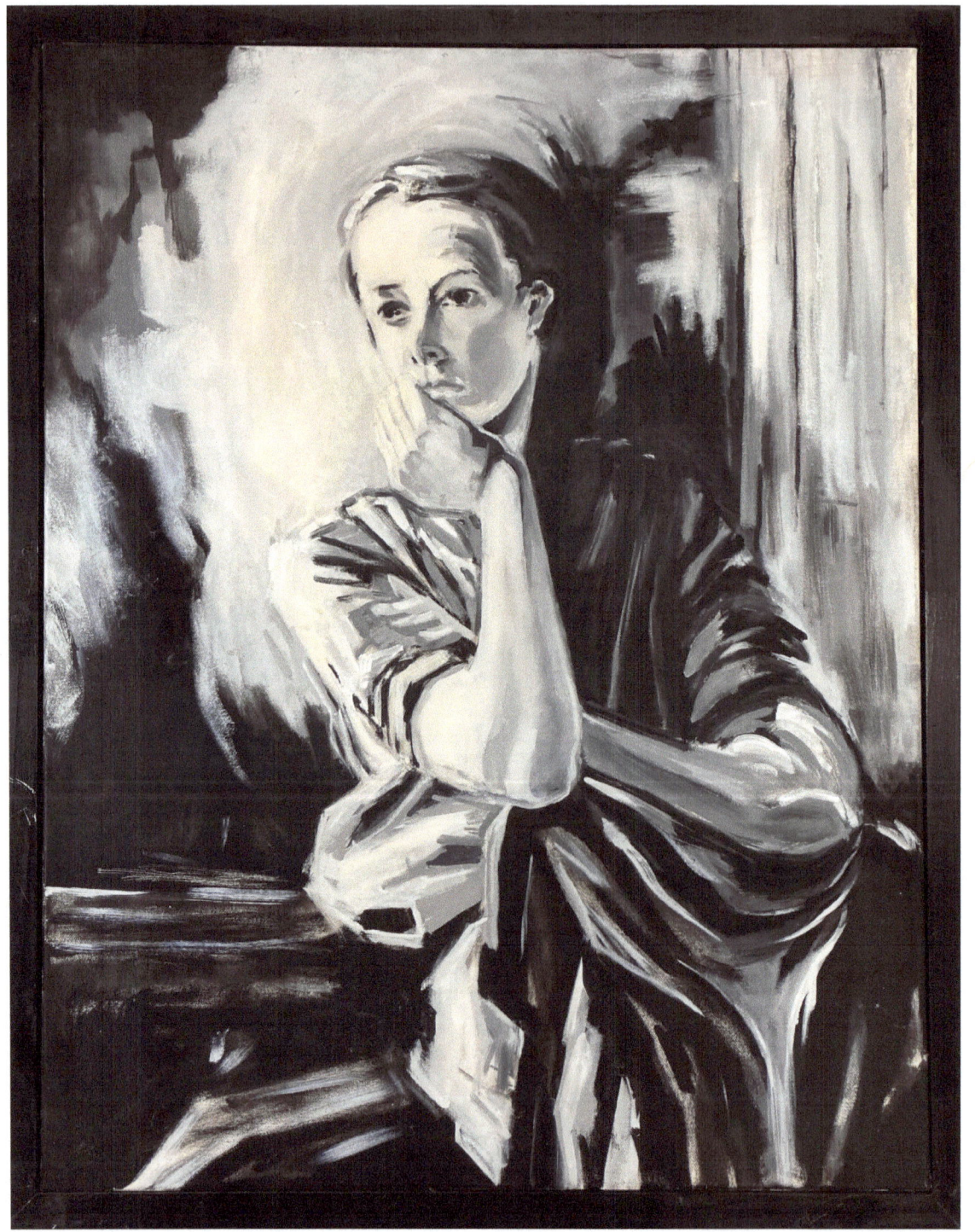

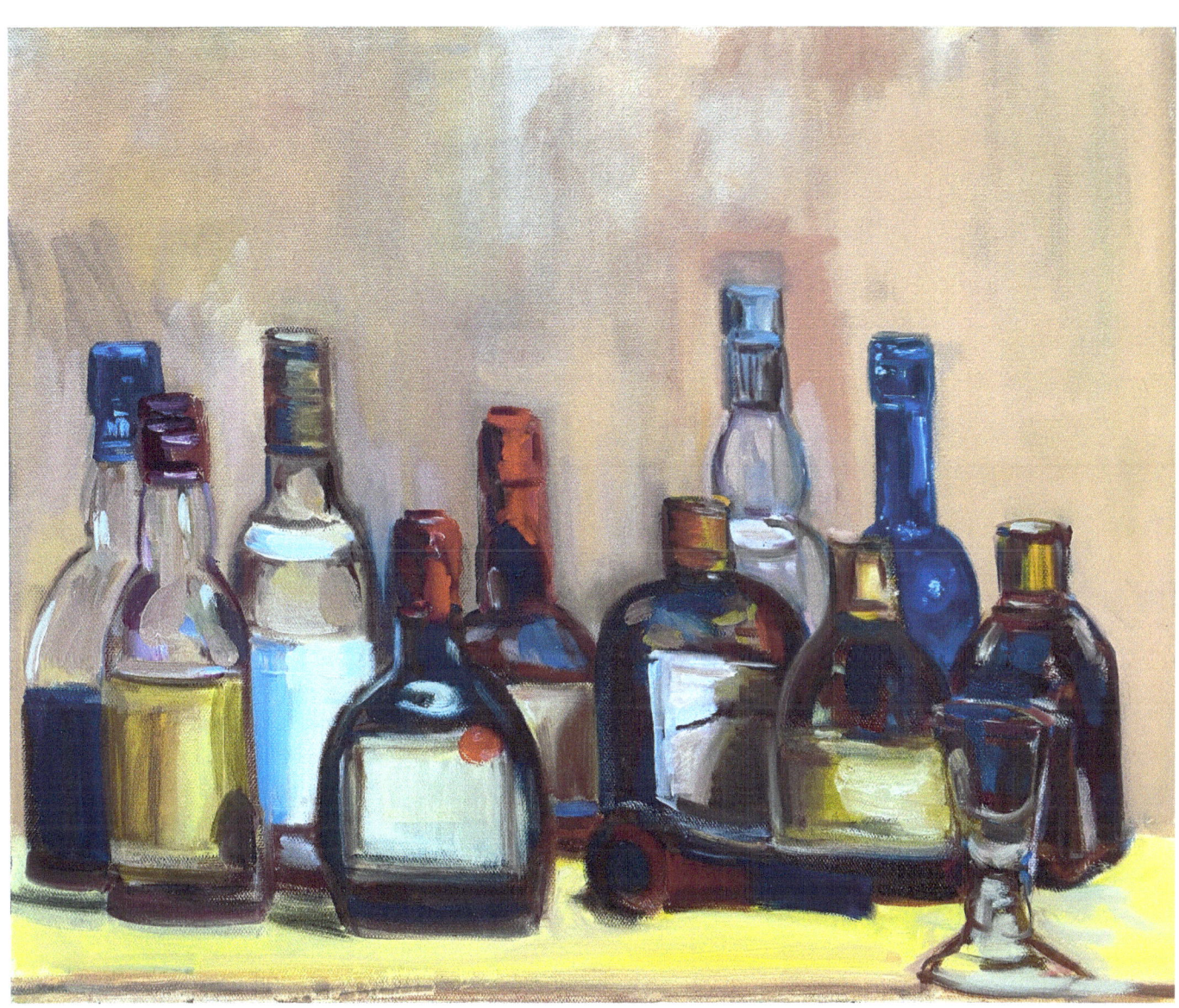

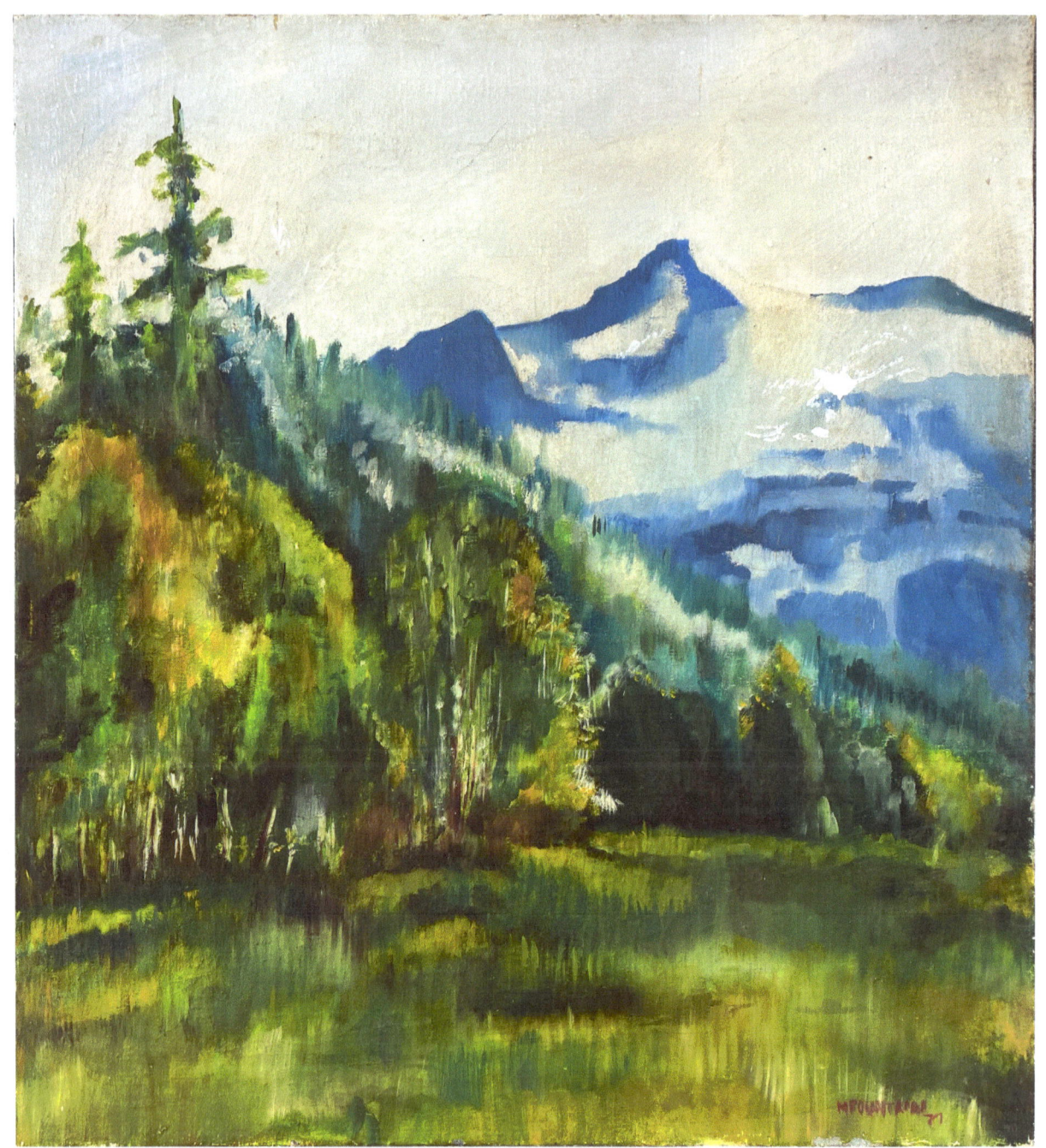

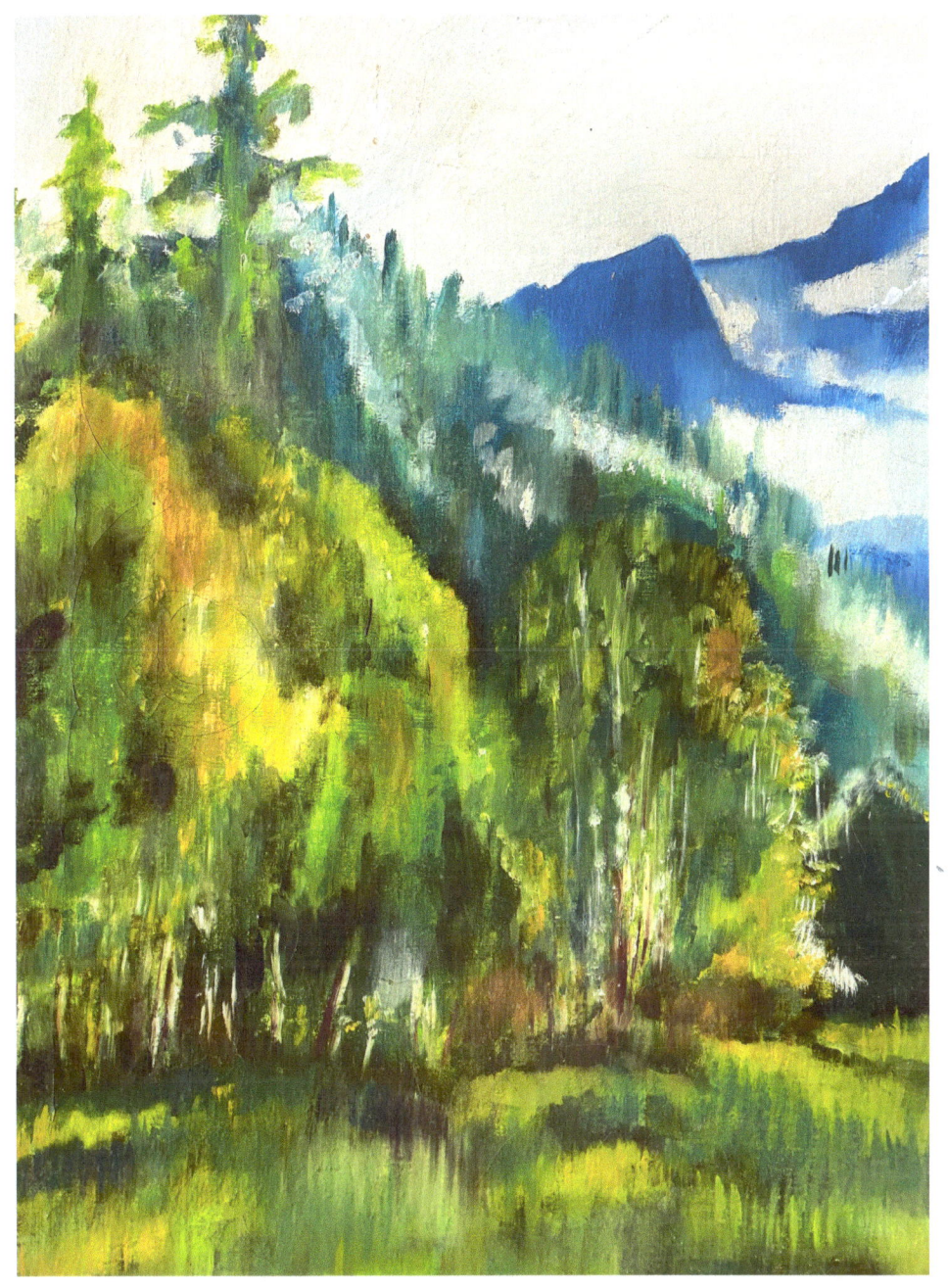

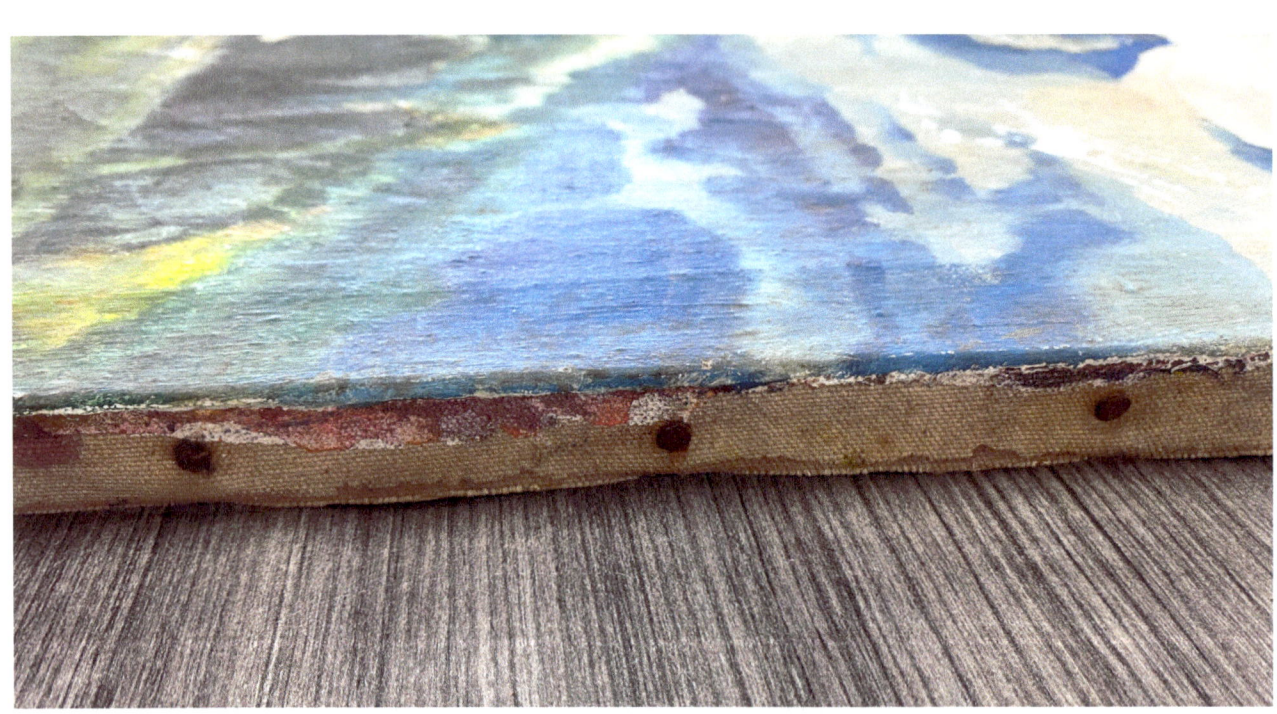

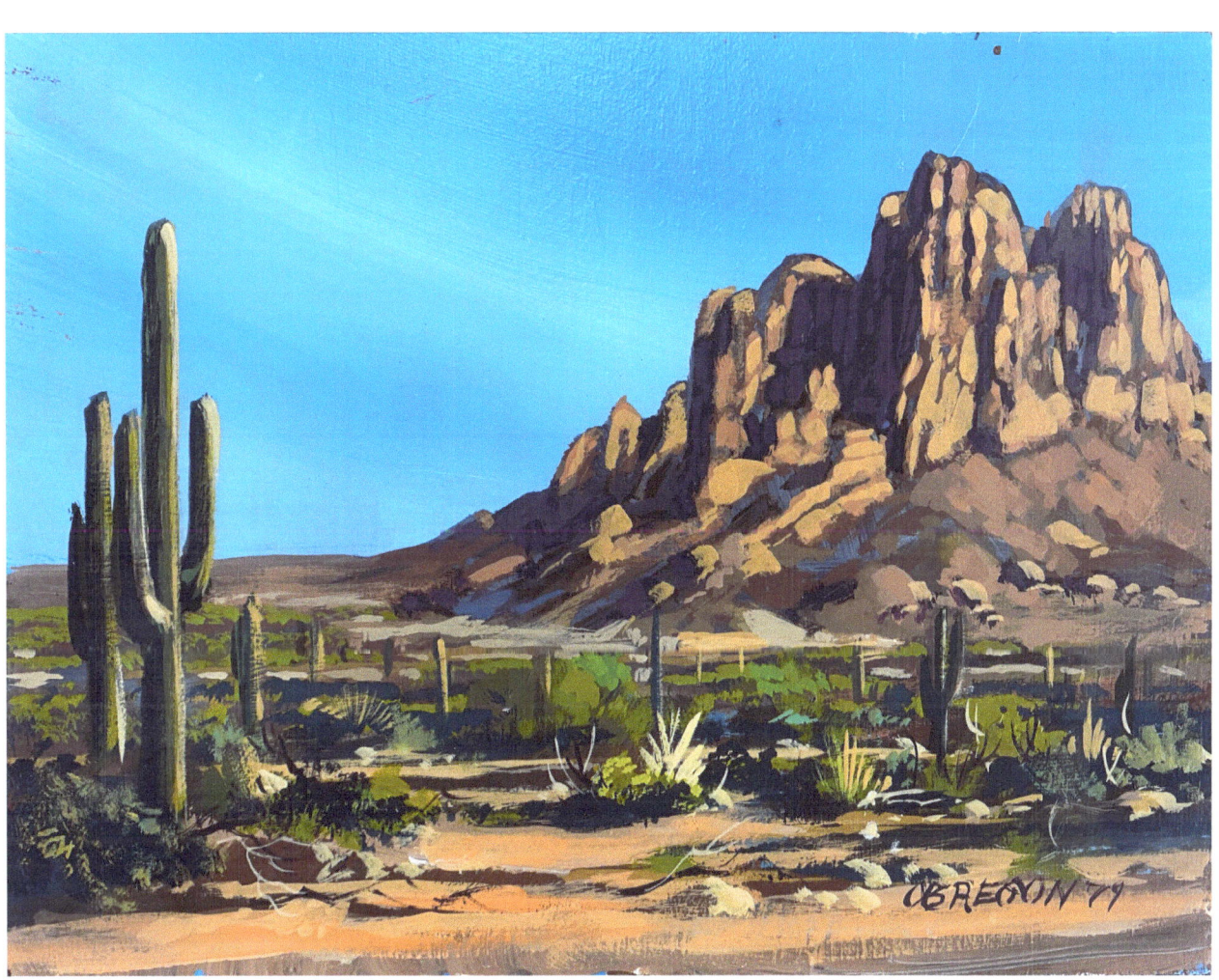

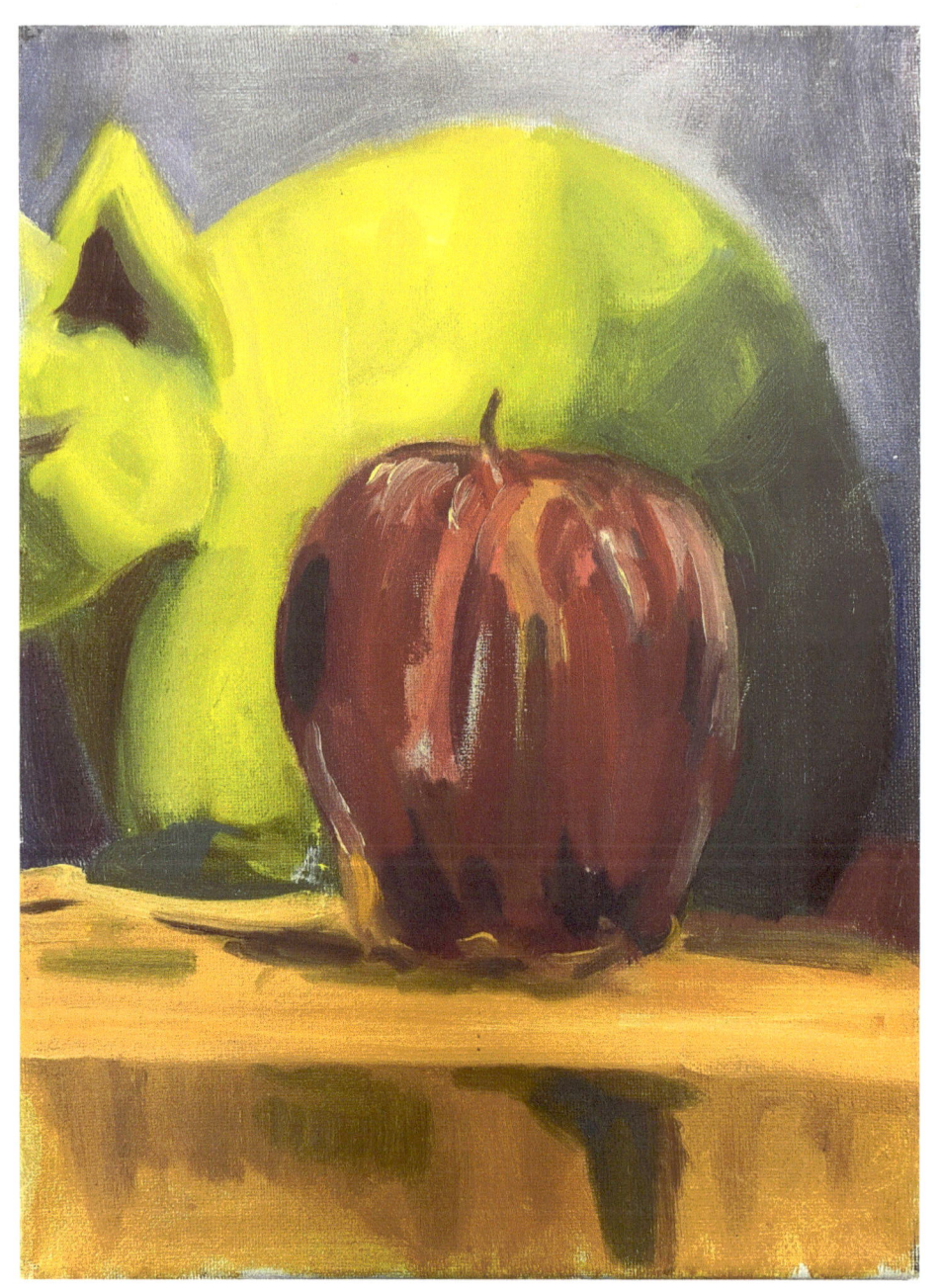

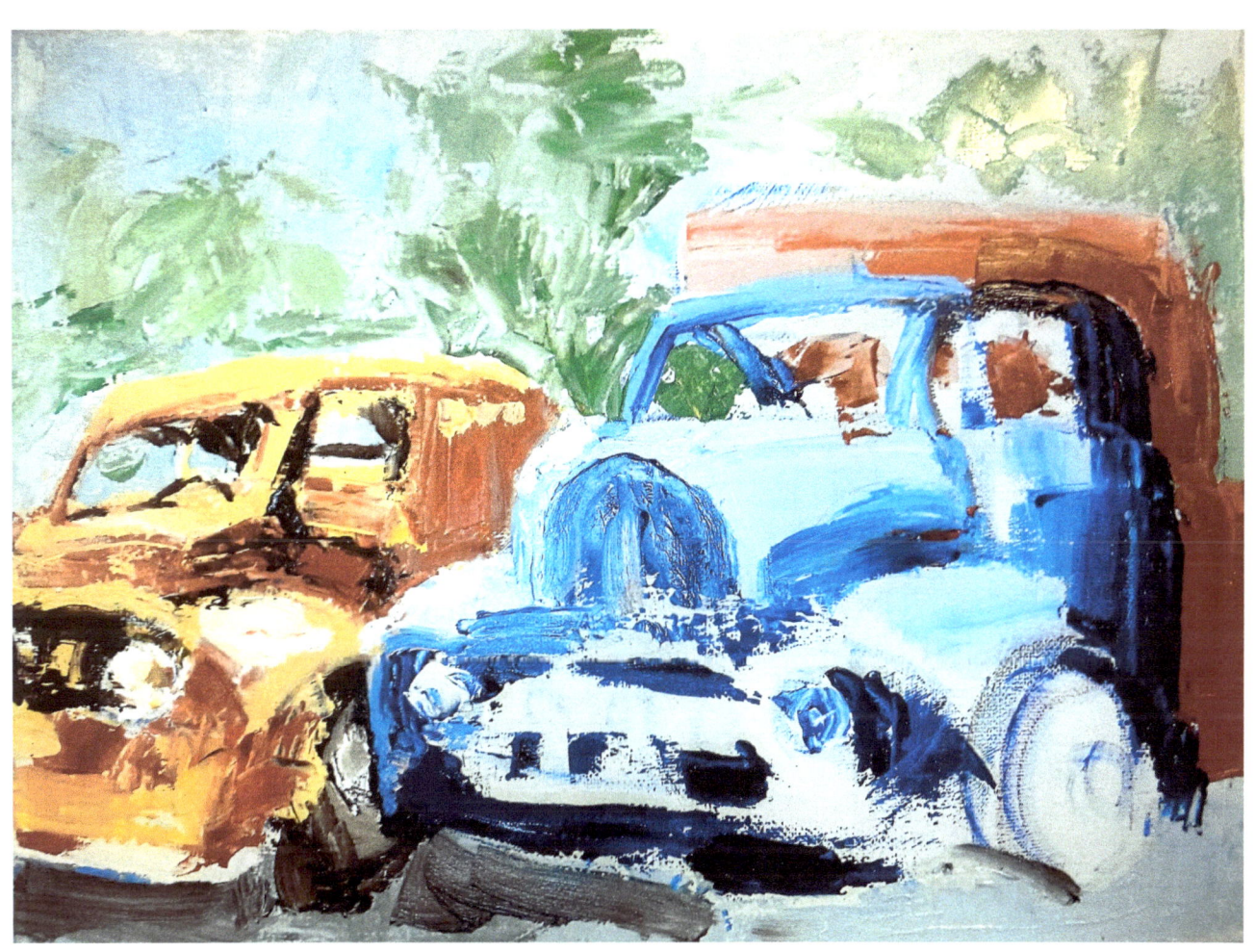

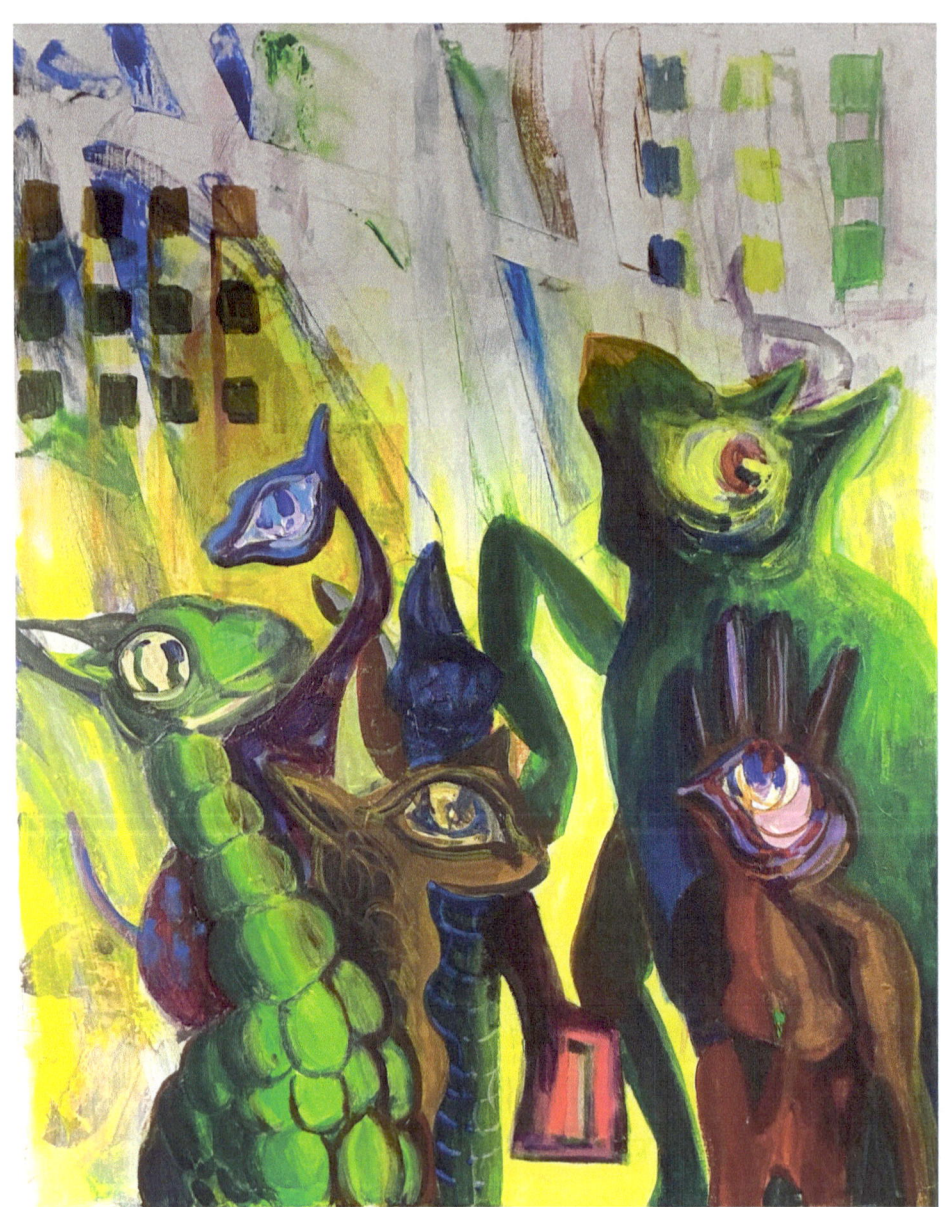

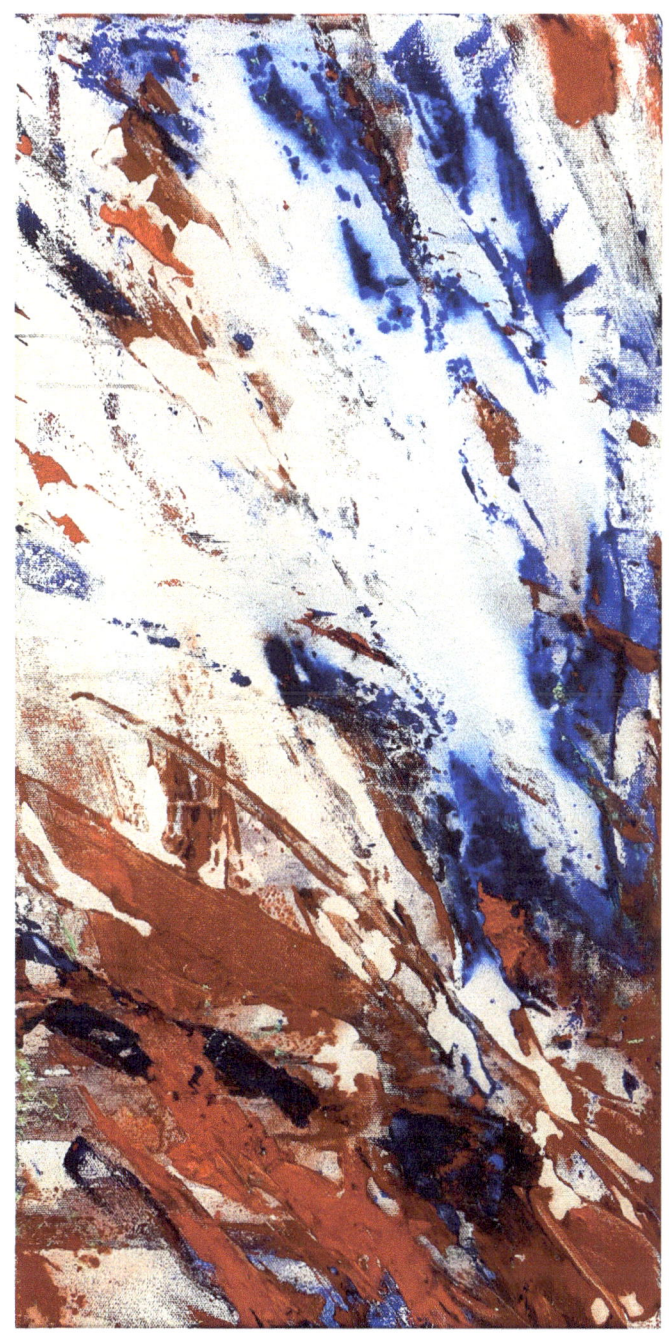

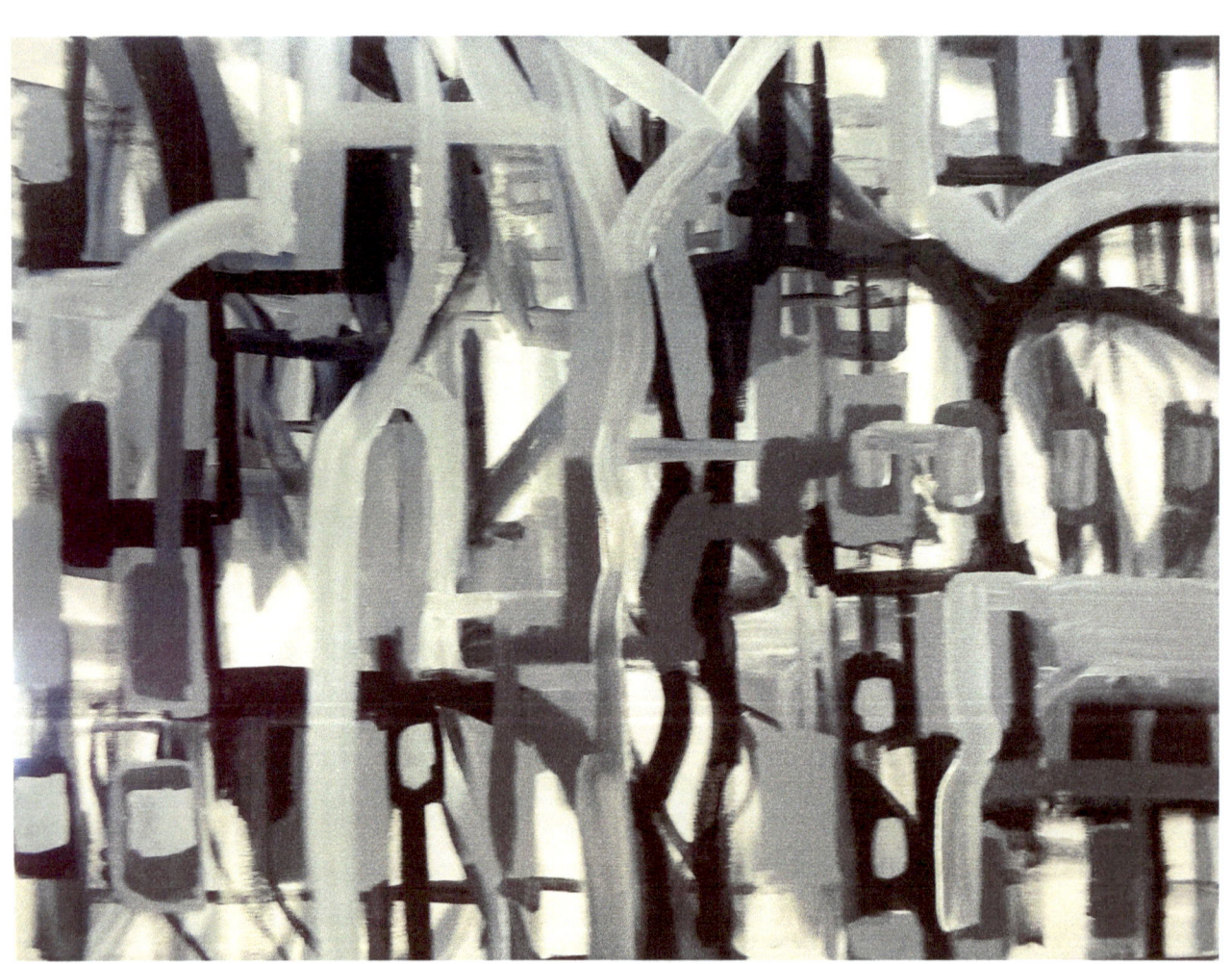

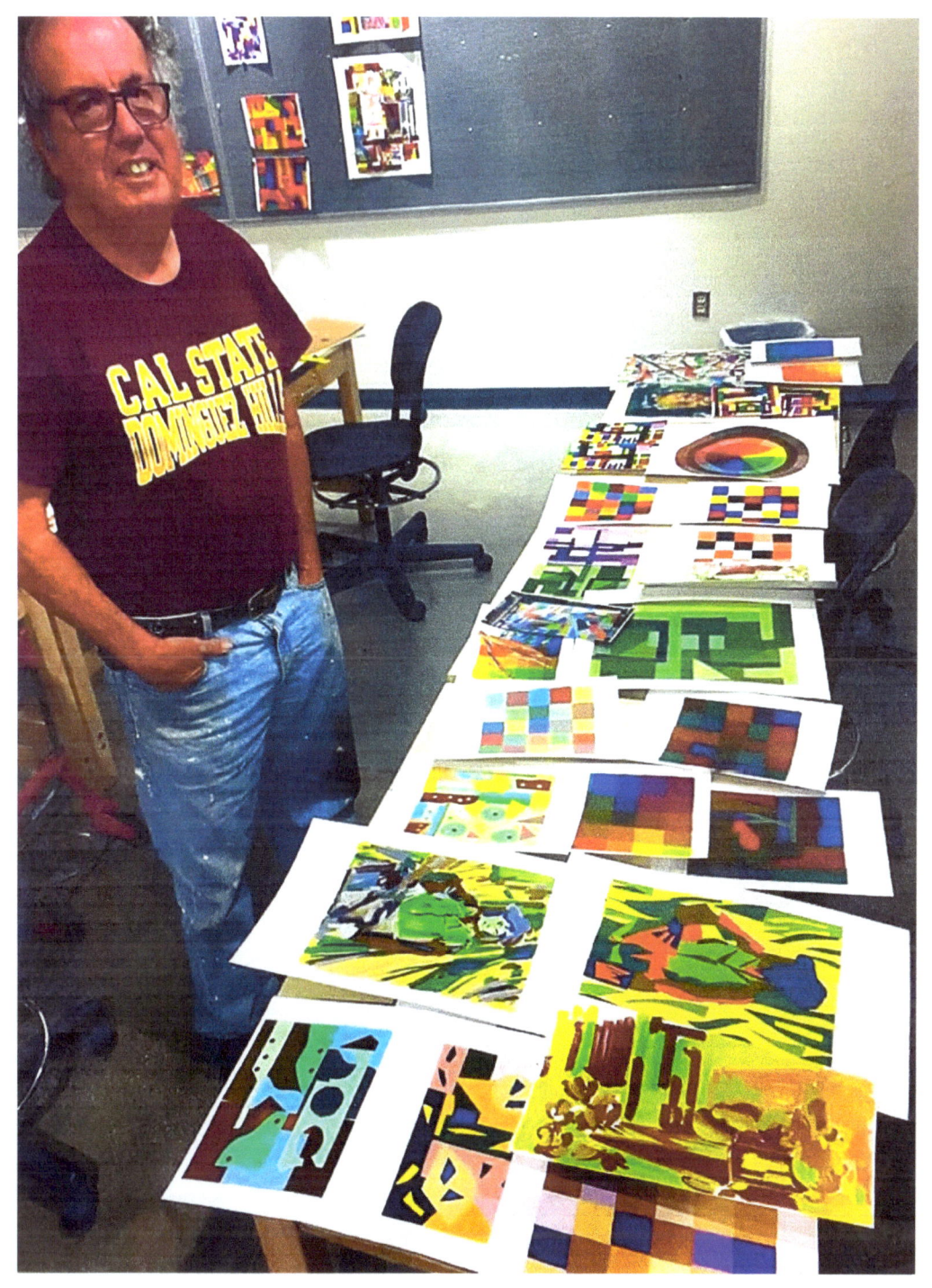

ABOUT ME

I have been a resident of Southern California my entire life and an art student for many years. The work in this collection dates from 1966 to the present. I received a B.A. in Art from Cal State Dominguez Hills. I would like to thank my wife Teresa for her support in my journey in the Art world. I hope that you enjoy my Art.